KARTCHNER
CAVERNS

KARTCHNER CAVERNS

How
Two
Cavers
Discovered
and Saved
One of the
Wonders
of the
Natural
World

**NEIL
MILLER**

The
University
of Arizona
Press

Tucson

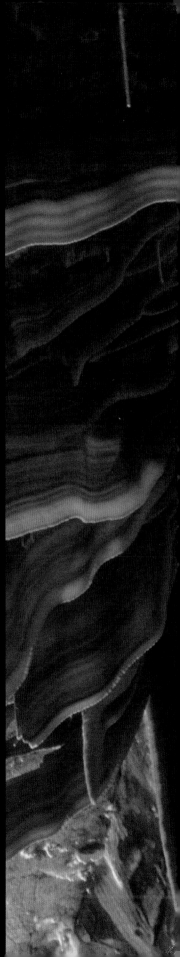

For Paul Brouillette

———————————

The University of Arizona Press
© 2008 Neil Miller
All rights reserved

Library of Congress Cataloging-in-Publication Data appear on the
last printed page of this book.

*Publication of this book is made possible in part by a generous
contribution from the Friends of Kartchner Caverns.*

Kartchner Caverns State Park® is a registered trademark of Arizona
State Parks.

This book is printed on acid-free, archival-quality paper.
Manufactured in Korea

13 12 11 10 09 08   6 5 4 3 2 1

CONTENTS

PART ONE **The Road to Xanadu**

ONE   The Discovery 3
TWO   Two Spelunkers 13
THREE   The Golden Age of Arizona Caving 21
FOUR   Exploring Xanadu 29
FIVE   Playing for Time 51
SIX   Encountering the Kartchners 63

PART TWO **The Making of Kartchner Caverns**

SEVEN   Lewis and Clark in Tucson 77
EIGHT   The Years in the Wilderness 95
NINE   The Stars Line Up 117
TEN   From Desert Outpost to State Park 139
ELEVEN   Epilogue 167

Acknowledgments 185
Timeline 187
People Interviewed 189
Notes 191
Bibliography 205
Index 209

The memory of a cave I used to know was always in my mind, with its lofty passages, its silence and solitude, its shrouding gloom, its sepulchral echoes, its fleeting lights, and more than all, its sudden revelations.

MARK TWAIN
Innocents Abroad

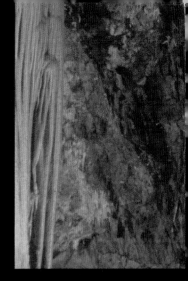

PART ONE

The
Road
to Xanadu

RANDY TUFTS AND GARY TENEN were always looking for holes in the ground, and on a Saturday in November 1974, they found one. The two young men left Tucson at about one o'clock in the afternoon in Tufts's red Rambler and headed east on the interstate toward the Whetstone Mountains. It was going to be a short trip, just following up a hunch. They didn't bother to bring much caving equipment. They took with them miners' hard hats, which attached to their heads by a chin strap, and carried a hammer and chisels, some rope, and a few crumpled packages of M&Ms and other snacks in their packs. The yellow-white gas flame of carbide lanterns, affixed to their helmets, would provide their only source of light.

Clouds hovered above them in the enormous Arizona sky, but the monsoon rains, with their displays of desert pyrotechnics, wouldn't return until July. Randy Tufts, who for most of his life kept voluminous journals and diaries, never marked the date of that particular caving trip in his notebooks. When he wrote about it years later, he described the day as "an overcast, cool November afternoon" and "date unknown." There were five Saturdays that November; it could have been any one of them.

The Whetstones were Randy Tufts and Gary Tenen's caving territory. Few of the other spelunkers in Tucson's Escabrosa Grotto, the local caving club, had much interest in exploring the isolated mountain range. The Whetstones loomed harsh and uninviting, known primarily for their white-tailed deer and javelinas—the wild, sharp-tusked mammals that look like pigs and dine on prickly pear cactus. It was in these mountains where the Apaches hid out and ambushed military patrols during the Indian wars of the 1870s, where, a decade later, the legendary Wyatt Earp faced down his enemies after his brother Morgan was shot dead at a billiard table in a Tombstone saloon. Over the years, little mining had taken place in the Whetstones, and there were few entry roads; the Whetstones were an obscure, almost forgotten country, even if they were only an hour or so drive from Tucson.

ONE

The Discovery

The Kartchner landscape in the Whetstone Mountains (Gary Tenen)

But, as Tufts and Tenen knew, the Whetstones possessed all the geologic elements ideal for the formation of caves: limestone, natural faults, and water. What they didn't know was that that day—while the attentions of their caving colleagues back at the Tucson grotto were focused elsewhere, on the Grand Canyon, on Mexico, on the Santa Ritas to the south—they would discover something extraordinary.

Lately, however, their caving expeditions hadn't brought them much luck. They'd been searching high up in the more rugged areas of the Whetstones, in places like French Joe Canyon and Dry Canyon. It was at French Joe that Tenen had almost gotten killed, rappelling down a cliff in search of an opening in the limestone face; Tufts saved his life. On those trips, they had ignored the scrubby foothills of the east face, covered with mesquite trees, barrel and prickly pear cactus, and ocotillo whose spiny tentacles make it look more like a sea creature than a desert plant. These gentler lower hills were simply too small to contain caves of any size, or so they thought. Mostly, the two cavers stayed on higher ground, exploring hundreds of little holes in the ground filled with packrat nests and finding nothing.

But on that November day they took a different approach. Seven years before, in the summer of 1967, while still in high school, Tufts

THE ROAD TO XANADU

had gone on a caving foray to the Whetstones with his uncle and two friends. On that occasion, in the Whetstone foothills, the group had stumbled upon a sinkhole, a natural depression usually formed by the collapse of the roof of a cave room. The sinkhole was in a low spot, almost invisible due to the contours of the rocky hills. But one of Tufts's companions, Steve Wade, had managed to pick it out. "There's a hell of a hole here," Wade shouted, and the group had scrambled down the twelve- to fifteen-foot-deep "sink." There, they found themselves in a small entryway, with a skull-and-crossbones and a cross carved on the wall and cactus spines and packrat dung littering the floor; they were evidently not the first who had made it into the sinkhole. In the midst of a jumble of large boulders, the visitors noticed a narrow crack descending parallel to the bedrock wall. But they never bothered to explore it, doubting that the crack led anywhere. Tufts marked the spot in his small blue notebook, calling it "Wade's Cave." Then he put the map in a drawer and ignored it for seven years.

Now, in the autumn of 1974, while hiking with his girlfriend, Randy Tufts had come upon the sinkhole again, in those very foothills of the east face that he and Tenen had been passing by so casually on their caving expeditions for many weeks and months. This time, he noticed what appeared to be a collapsed entrance on the other side of the U-shaped hill. The fact that there might be two entrances piqued Tufts's interest. Perhaps the hill was more porous than he had imagined.

The sinkhole on the east end of the Whetstones (Gary Tenen)

A week after his rediscovery, Tufts persuaded Tenen, one his room-mates in a "group house" just off the campus of the University of Arizona in Tucson, to drive out with him and investigate. He wondered if he and the caving companions of his teenage years might have dismissed the hill containing the sinkhole too easily. It was definitely worth another look.

On their arrival, they checked out the second possible entrance, but quickly discovered it didn't lead anywhere. They turned back to "Wade's Cave." The pair lowered themselves into the sinkhole, quickly finding themselves inside the same dry and dusty entrance that Tufts had visited seven years before. Here, they encountered the skull-and-crossbones on the wall, as well as broken stalactites and footprints, and the ten-inch-wide crack. They could still see daylight through the overhang of the sinkhole above them. But something was different from that day back in 1967. This time, the air seemed to be moving. Through the crack, a faint current of air was coming up from among the rocks, warm and moist and enticing, with the musty smell of bats.

"There has got to be a cave here!" exclaimed an excited Tenen.

Tenen, who at 5'7" was the smaller of the two, wasted no time squeezing through the crack. Back home in Tucson, he had been practicing navigating his way through narrow spaces by wiggling through his closet coat hangers. Tufts, at six feet tall and 170 pounds, had a little more trouble: he had to fully exhale to twist through the opening, nearly turning a somersault on the way. Five feet down they came upon a chamber about the size of a living room, just high enough to stand in. Next to it, linked by another short crawl, was a similar room with a lower ceiling and an eight-inch stalagmite in the middle of the floor, expanding at the tip. Tufts, a space enthusiast, thought the formation resembled the footpad of the Apollo lunar module spacecraft.

But the small volume of the two rooms just didn't account for the breeze. The air current had to be coming from someplace else, somewhere farther, deeper underground. In the second room, Tufts and Tenen shined their lights through all the nooks and crannies. They didn't see anything. Just when they were about to give up, hidden underneath a small flowstone shelf in the back corner, Tufts noticed a low, tight crawlway, ten inches high and two feet across, twisting into the darkness in the direction of the air current.

They followed it. Tufts crawled on his belly for an agonizing twenty feet, scraping his ribs and elbows and pushing his pack in front of him along the rough gravel; Tenen inched his way behind him. The passage ended abruptly at a rock barrier.

However, in the center of that barrier was a grapefruit-sized hole, a "blowhole," in caver's parlance, large enough to see through with only one eye. When Tufts shined his carbide lamp through the hole, the swirling air behind blew out the flame almost immediately. For a caver, that was the road sign, a sure clue that there was some kind of passage beyond, a passage that most likely led somewhere. The men lay there for two hours hacking away at the wall with a two-pound sledgehammer and chisel, one person going at it at a time, trading off when their arms got tired. It was a tedious and exhausting job, made even more difficult by the tight, constricted space in which they were forced to work. Sweat was pouring off them in the underground air whose humidity approached 100 percent. Tenen was becoming more and more frustrated at the wall's dogged refusal to yield to his persuasions. He swung his hammer back to give it a good pounding and wound up walloping himself in the forehead instead. That happened more than once. But the two men kept at it, focused and persistent.

It was all routine, even if hundreds of pounds of earth were pressing down on their heads, even though the ceiling might potentially collapse at any moment, even if they were surrounded by a sea of darkness and had no idea what lay in front of them. Tufts and Tenen didn't worry about those things. For cavers, it was all in a day's work.

With the constant pressure and pounding, they managed to widen the hole ever so slightly. The air behind it kept moving as if a giant bellows lay on the other side of that wall, as if the earth was taking deep breaths, accompanying them as they worked. Finally, Tenen took off his shirt and was able to squeeze through the expanded opening. He chipped away from the other side so Tufts could just make it through, grunting and scraping. The ceiling was higher on the far side of the blowhole, three feet now, and they could maneuver more easily there. Hackberry seeds and bat guano (excrement) covered the floor. On their hands and knees, they made their way for about 250 feet along a corridor where they could stand up, and where there were no more signs of previous human visitors. The "stand-up passage" was the first indication that they had found something significant.

They continued down a corridor that appeared to be a main route. Wet, glistening stalactites, conical in shape, and hollow, filament-like soda straws hung down from the ceiling; the two cavers crouched to avoid bumping their heads and breaking off formations. The floor became a thin crust of flowstone, no longer the rough gravel of the earlier portions. Water was dripping everywhere. It was warm, about sixty-eight degrees, but it seemed warmer; the air was dank and humid, so humid that their skin glistened and they could see their own breath. The damp air smelled like a basement of a house that had been shut up since the beginning of time. They passed a gleaming three-foot calcite scroll and took a close look at a distinctive boulder as they passed—

Randy Tufts squeezes through the blowhole.

they needed to remember it as a landmark to find their way back out. As the two men pushed on and the distance seemed to only expand, their hearts were racing.

"It's got to stop, right?" Tenen kept asking.

But it didn't stop.

Tufts and Tenen entered a larger room that appeared to extend ahead for quite a while. A ceiling decorated with brightly colored orange stalactites curved eight feet above them, and piles of pungent bat guano—five feet in diameter, in some cases—blocked their path. The oppressive damp closed in, and it was hard to see. The range of their headlamps was only fifty feet or so; everything beyond that was shrouded in shadow and mystery. The two men couldn't tell how far the chamber went or where it might lead. When they reached a flat expanse of mud, they stopped for a moment, turning out their lamps, and sat in the great empty blackness—as black as anything they had ever seen. It was impossible to see their hands in front of their faces. The only sounds were the meditative tick-tock of water dripping from the tips of the stalactites and soda straws to the floor. After a few minutes the cavers re-lit their lights. Everything was as astonishing as it had seemed before: the glistening orange flowstone streaming down from the ceil-

Soda straws, stalactities, and stalagmites in what Randy Tufts always referred to as "The Cave" (K.I. Day, Arizona State Parks)

THE ROAD TO XANADU

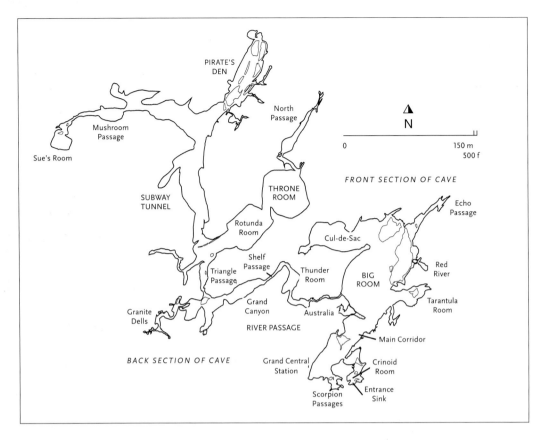

Layout of Kartchner Caverns
(Arizona State Parks)

ing, the water droplets shimmering on the cave floor, the darkness and mystery just beyond the range of their carbide lanterns, beckoning them, perhaps cautioning them as well.

They wanted to go on and on to see what might lie beyond, how far it continued, if it opened up farther. But Tufts and Tenen prided themselves on not being the kind of cavers who took unnecessary risks. A realistic sense of their situation began to hit them. Good caving practice requires that a caver always be accompanied by a minimum of two other people and must carry three sources of light as an extra precaution. Tufts and Tenen had violated the first rule of caving; most importantly, no one had any idea where they were. It was already getting late. If anything happened, if they lost their way or fell into a pit or got stuck in a crawlway, they might never be found. Cave rescues often took days.

"We'd better get out of here!" they said, almost simultaneously. The two retraced their steps, crawling back the way they came. As they

Stalactites in the mud flats
area (K.L. Day, Arizona
State Parks)

climbed out of the sinkhole, dirty and tired, the daylight and the fresh, cool air hit them with an exhilarating sharpness, as if they were leaving a movie theater after a matinee. It always felt that way when they came out of a cave, but this time there was an extra punch.

Tufts and Tenen walked downhill to the car, with the pale-blue panorama of the nearby mountain ranges, the Dragoons, the Mules, the Mustangs, and the Huachucas, in front of them. They were astonished to find a cave in this part of the Whetstones, barely eight miles from the interstate that snakes through southern Arizona and half a mile from State Highway 90, the route that Tucson commuters took every day to go to work at the army post at Fort Huachuca. From the sinkhole, they could actually hear the sound of cars driving along the highway. Most amazingly, what they had discovered was a virgin cave, pristine, dripping wet, totally alive, with the stalactites, stalagmites, and soda straws still growing with each drop of water. It was evident that no one had ever been beyond the blowhole before. How much more cave was there? What else would they find? Whom could they tell about it?

They would come back the following week, they decided, there was no doubt about that. But little did Tufts and Tenen realize that this was only the beginning, the start of a grand adventure that would absorb them for the next twenty-five years and more, that would transform their lives and the geography of American caving. Although they didn't know it on that chilly November day—there was so much more remaining to see and explore—they had stumbled upon one of the last undiscovered treasures of the American West.

WHEN RANDY TUFTS was a high school student, he sneaked into Colossal Cave, a popular tourist attraction on the fringes of Tucson that had been an inspiration for scores of young Arizona cavers. Tufts entered the cave from a back entrance, known as the Bandits' Escape Route. Like the Whetstone Mountains, Colossal had been the hiding place for numerous fugitives from the law, most famously four bandits who had stolen $3,000–$72,000 (estimates vary) from a mail train in the 1880s; legend has it that the loot remains hidden somewhere in the cave. The young caver wandered around, exploring serpentine passages, gazing at towering formations with names like Crystal Forest and Kingdom of the Elves. But after a couple of hours, he was unable to find his way out. He was confused and seemed to be going around in circles. Then, as he turned a corner, he heard the echoing voices of a tour group. He realized that his only hope of escape was to join up with them. But a scruffy teenager, wearing a caver's helmet and covered in dust and grime, didn't blend in among a group of eager, wide-eyed visitors from Iowa and Kansas. Tufts was brought to the office of the cave's operator Joe Maierhauser to explain himself. He was trespassing, of course, and hadn't bought an admission ticket. Maierhauser, who knew his father, let him off with a stern lecture.

Bruce Randall Tufts had always dreamed of discovering a cave that no one had ever seen before. As a youngster growing up in the 1950s on Tucson's east side, he spent much of his time digging fallout shelters in his backyard. In the fourth grade, he read *Five Boys in a Cave,* an enthralling British "boys' book" about an expedition in which a group of schoolboys find themselves lost and cut off from one another in a maze of underground passages. His uncle Harry Walker, his mother's brother—a chemist, caver, and mountaineer—took him caving as a teenager in a number of "wild," undeveloped caves. In his high school yearbook, one of his classmates scribbled, "Bat guano to you, too! Don't get lost in any caves this summer!" At the University of Arizona, where

Two Spelunkers

he matriculated in 1966, Tufts majored in geology, a subject as near to his caving heart as anything he could find.

Tufts, twenty-six at the time of the discovery of the cave, was a native Tucsonan, tall, with a mustache and soon-to-be-thinning hair, an easy manner, a philosophical bent, and a lifelong love for corny jokes and puns. He came by his sense of adventure naturally. His mother Carol, a social activist well-known in Tucson, was the daughter of a "mining man" who, according to family lore, left home at fourteen and participated in the Rawhide, Nevada, silver strike of 1907; he brought the family from California to northern Arizona during the Great Depression to work an old mining claim. In her undergraduate days at the University of Arizona, Carol had been an editor of the campus newspaper *The Wildcat*. His father, Pete, came to Tucson from New York City as a young man for his asthma. Pete worked as a radio announcer, sometimes making up the play-by-play for the Class C Tucson Cowboys' out-of-town baseball games that he broadcast in the days when information would dribble in by telephone, and wound up in the advertising and public relations business. Pete's father was said to have been the first person to hike the Appalachian Trail from Maine to Georgia.

In many ways, Randy Tufts and Gary Tenen were very different. Tenen, twenty-three when he and Tufts drove out to the Whetstones that November day, had never dreamed of caves. Wiry, bearded, Jewish, a self-styled "doer," he had spent winters in the dry air of Tucson as a child due to respiratory problems, but otherwise had grown up in a Chicago apartment house. (He was so sickly as a child that at one point, so the family story goes, his parents brought snow on a platter to his sickbed so he could see it.) He returned to Tucson to go to the University of Arizona. His father, who came to the States from Germany at the end of World War I, was a successful furrier who at one point played the violin with the Chicago Symphony Orchestra. If Tufts was outgoing, with a laid-back Southwest charm, Tenen was more introverted and intense. Often he would be quiet in conversation for a long time and then burst out in impassioned argument. He was self-effacing and modest, but he was always listening.

But these differences seemed to complement one another—Tenen, pragmatic, determined, sometimes impulsive, and Tufts, the visionary, the dreamer. Later in life, Tenen became a successful businessman and Tufts a planetary scientist. It all seemed metaphoric: Tenen was focused on the earth, while Tufts was looking at the stars.

One thing they had in common was that they were both thoughtful, with a scientific bent. Tufts was the geology major who would later move from the study of limestone on planet Earth to the icy crust of Jupiter's moon Europa. Tenen was interested in entomology (the study of insects) and had seriously considered becoming an entomologist; he always walked with his head down, looking for bugs. They also shared an interest in politics and world affairs and a strong sense of idealism and social commitment; in that way, they were very much the product of their times.

On the first caving trip that Tufts and Tenen took together, the two men and a group of friends went to Pyeatt Cave, within the grounds of the military post at Fort Huachuca. Soon after, at the Cave of the Bells, in Sawmill Canyon in the Santa Rita Mountains near Tucson, they discovered a previously unknown loop route and a crystal-lined passage. In the less well-traveled Whetstones, they made another discovery: a narrow cavern they named Red Cave, where they came upon a Hohokam Indian cave shrine, featuring turquoise, bone beads, arrow shafts, and an intact bowl made of red clay, some eight hundred years old. The two cavers notified the Arizona State University Museum in Tempe, where some of the artifacts reside today.

Tufts and Tenen were medium-level cavers, not taking as many risks or going on as far-flung expeditions as some, but careful and attentive. When they searched for caves, they were methodical: they each would stand a few hundred feet apart and start climbing a hill, slowly examining every crack and crevice to see if it might lead anywhere underground. Then the two would return to the bottom of the hill, move a few feet to the right (or to the left), and hike up again and again in a grid-like fashion, always remaining the same distance apart. After each caving trip, they marked deposits of limestone in dark gray on their geologic maps for future reference. If there was limestone, there was always the possibility of finding a cave.

"They had a scientific understanding of all this," said John Kromko, a friend and next-door neighbor who accompanied Tufts and Tenen on that first trip to Pyeatt Cave. "Randy would say, 'There must be an opening here because of the wind' or because of something about the limestone. He was like an oil explorer."

It was Tufts who introduced Tenen to the art of spelunking, and Tenen took to it immediately. He soon became as good a caver as his friend, even a little better when it came to climbing and rope work.

"Either you love it or hate it," Tenen says of caving. "I loved it."

Caving was a perfect fit for Tenen. In his younger days, he never cared for organized sports, but he did enjoy physical activity. The transplanted Chicagoan was a bit of a loner, and part of the appeal of caving for him was the solitude, the peacefulness. At the same time, the scientific aspect attracted his intellectual curiosity. And he liked the atmosphere of a cave, too—the smells, the predictable and soothing sounds of dripping water, the transcendent quiet of it all.

Tufts and Tenen met in 1970 at a political meeting when they were both students at the University of Arizona (UA). The two drew closer when they volunteered together at The Cup, the once-a-week coffee house, located at the Campus Christian Center, where local musicians played folk and bluegrass, and patrons drank hot chocolate and cider. (Singer Linda Ronstadt, a native Tucsonan, used to perform there before Tufts and Tenen came on the scene.) The next year, along with fellow student Brad Barber, they became roommates in a large "group house" on Tucson's University Avenue near the UA campus. Now torn down, it resembled a frat house—at one time they tried to receive university recognition as a mock fraternity, even creating a humorous sign in gold letters and putting it out in front—and its interior walls were a maze of geometric patterns, painted by a local artist and roommate.

During this period the University of Arizona and the neighborhood around it began to change dramatically. When Tufts and Tenen's friend John Kromko came there from Temple University in Philadelphia to work on his Ph.D. in the mid-1960s, he was shocked at how "straight and conservative" the UA was. At the housing office, he found ads that said "Colored need not apply"; women had to inform the university before they married. Within a few years, though, with the Vietnam War raging and the military draft hanging over the heads of the male students, everything was transformed. The student senate, where Kromko and Tufts met, was still composed, as in the past, of fraternity and sorority presidents, but now the men sported long hair and camouflage attire and army jackets. Anti-war rallies mobilized the campus, drawing thousands of students to the mall; student leaders would call a meeting and five hundred students would show up almost instantly. The old business district on North Fourth Avenue, not far from the university, became a small-scale version of Berkeley's Telegraph Avenue, featuring coffeehouses, bookstores, shops selling incense and beads, and runaways hanging out on street corners. The city even had its own full-fledged riot when police tried to force "street people" away from an area adjoining the UA campus.

It was a tumultuous time in Tucson, as in so many college towns around the country, and Tufts and Tenen were in the thick of it. At the UA, Tenen was a prominent campus activist, whose bushy beard, frizzy hair, and fondness for army surplus attire made him look a little like Fidel Castro. He was one of the organizers of the Free Clinic and the Switchboard Hotline and took part in a number of anti-war demonstrations. He was said to be on the police list of the "Ten most active campus radicals" in Tucson. On one occasion during those days, Tenen recalls, a policeman pulled him over for a routine traffic stop; he looked at his

Randy Tufts and other victorious candidates after Tufts's election as UA student body president in 1971 (*Tucson Citizen*)

license, frowned, and said quizzically, "That name sounds familiar." But the officer didn't pursue it.

Tufts was a campus figure as well and, by the time he left, probably the most well-known student personality at the UA. But he tended to work through the system. When passions ran high as UA students rallied against the killings of anti-war protesters by the National Guard at Ohio's Kent State University in May 1970, he served as a "peace marshal." "I just couldn't live with myself if something like that [the Kent State shootings] happened in Tucson," he told his mother. Tufts had been a student senator for two years when, in the spring of 1971, he was elected president of the student body (Associated Students of the University of Arizona or ASUA).

Tufts wasn't the obvious person to be a campus leader. He was a geology major, and geology majors weren't supposed to be articulate or outgoing; he wasn't entirely presentable either—his wardrobe largely consisted of two pairs of jeans, both worn at the knee. "No one had ever seen him in a sport coat and tie until that time," said his close friend and roommate Brad Barber. "A group of his friends got him cleaned up. They collected a bunch of money and took him shopping for clothes." A photo in the 1972 *Desert,* the college yearbook, shows Tufts with relatively neat long hair and mustache and button-down Oxford shirt, looking like the epitomal student government type with counterculture leanings.

But, if his fashion sense was lacking, clearly he had other virtues. "Randy had the ability to say one sentence that summed up everything," said Barber. "He had an innate sense of being able to think before he talked. He was, above all, thoughtful. He would sit and think about things. Then he would come up with an answer and do it." John Kromko saw him similarly. "He was very smooth, but not in a sleazy way," he said. "He put issues in terms that people could understand." These qualities, first developed in a church youth group while he was in high school (sometimes the minister would ask him to deliver sermons on Sunday morning) and refined during his tenure as student body president, would serve him well in the future when it came to advocating on behalf of the cave.

After his election, the local Nihilist Organization postered the campus with a broadside blasting the ASUA vote—Tufts had defeated his opponent by a substantial 1,717 to 1,265 votes—and noting snidely that "the newest group of junior administrators, freshly scrubbed and beaming, led by Randy Tufts, will soon sit at their desks to commence playing executive in the toy government." Tufts and his colleagues soon proved to be far from administration yes-men. They reformed the university committee system, insisting on greater student participation, and set up various student businesses from a charter airfare service to a summer storage facility to a bar. In the process, Tufts found himself challenging the newly appointed UA president John Paul Schaefer on a host of issues. "The basic battle between them was over student control of student funds," said Barber. "The university collected a student activity fee from all the students, but the students had no input as to where the money went. At first we thought Schaefer would be sympathetic. But students wanted to spend money on things like birth control clinics." Under Tufts's leadership they sued the Board of Regents to gain control of the student-owned bookstore profits and established a Student Services Corporation to fund student projects without administration approval or control.

The corporation's most well-known achievement was the opening of a bar called Merlin's at a former car dealership on North Fourth Avenue near campus, all of whose profits went toward various student organizations and activities. The bar, which the students essentially built from scratch and which had an Old English décor, was constantly packed and known for booking the most popular bands in Tucson; for a while, it supposedly sold more beer than any other bar in the state. Tufts essentially managed the place. But after a couple of years, as the spirit of the student movement of the 1960s and '70s began to fade, the bar languished and eventually shut its doors.

Tufts's role and many achievements as student body president made him a highly popular figure among many students, with a reputation for integrity and incorruptibility. "I don't think that I ever before or since met someone who wasn't in it for himself, like Randy," said Kromko, who served in the Arizona legislature from 1976 to 1990. Tufts's friends assumed he would go into politics, maybe become governor someday.

During this period of campus political involvement, Tufts's caving activities took a back seat. He was just too busy. But the dream of discovery, nourished through childhood and adolescence, always lurked in the background, ready to reassert itself when the chance came. And when caving began to fascinate his roommate Gary Tenen, the big-city boy and would-be entomologist who always walked with his head down, as if he were an experienced spelunker already, the opportunity had arrived.

THE 1960S AND '70S were the heyday of the environmental movement and the "outdoor revolution." A new consciousness about the environment was emerging, largely an outgrowth of the social movements
of the time. Edward Abbey's *Desert Solitaire,* published in 1968, extolled
the glories of wild places. In January 1970, President Richard M. Nixon
signed the National Environmental Policy Act into law, requiring that
federal agencies take into account the ecological effects of their actions.
April 22 of that year marked the first Earth Day, attracting millions of
people around the United States. At the same time, large numbers of
young people began to spend their weekends in various outdoor activities: hiking, camping, bicycling. Tucson, bounded by the serene beauty
of the Sonoran Desert and the majestic peaks of the Santa Catalina
Mountains, provided a perfect setting. The desert and mountains were
easily accessible, and the city's outskirts were an outdoor paradise of
trails over craggy ridges and hillsides covered with mesquite and palo
verde trees and cacti of all varieties—giant saguaro, spiny prickly pear,
and stout barrel cactus (described by Edward Abbey as "tall as a man
and fat as a keg of beer"). And just beneath some of that beautiful scen-
ery, particularly to the south and southeast of Tucson, limestone caves
could be found. Arizona didn't possess as many caves as other parts of
the country—at the time, it had an estimated 260 of them, compared to
Missouri's 4,825, Kentucky's 3,770, and New Mexico's 1,100. But in Arizona, a group of cavers—mostly, but not entirely, university students—
began exploring and discovering caves all over the state.

"It was the golden age of Arizona caving," said Tucson caver Bill
Peachey. "You could go out on weekends and find new caves. There were
few people and lots of land. So we divided up territory. There was a revolution in equipment. It was a passion that bonded people who wouldn't
normally be together—Ph.D.s and military people, for example. Everyone had a caving partner. That is how Randy and Gary began."

While caving might not be as glamorous as mountaineering or
deep-sea diving, it was something that anyone could do almost any-

THREE

The Golden Age of Arizona Caving

A long and delicate helictite growing parallel to the ceiling. Helictites are formed when water under pressure grows in varying directions. (Bob Buecher)

where with some of the same thrill and satisfaction. You didn't have to live near an ocean or a national park—the lonesome mountain valleys of Virginia and Kentucky and Arkansas were among the best places, really—or use fancy equipment. You could explore the unknown and not have to venture far from home. For some, the appeal was to find a virgin cave, never before glimpsed by human eyes, as Randy Tufts dreamed of doing. For others, the allure was the sheer beauty of what they saw underground—the noble stalagmites rising from the floor; the tiny and delicate helictites twisting in all directions and seeming to defy gravity; the richly colored and textured cave draperies. Still others were drawn by the physical aspect of caving, expanding the way you used your body, utilizing muscles you wouldn't otherwise employ in an effort to force your way through narrow squeezes and tight spots. Bruises and scraped knees and elbows were the trophies of a day spent underground. And for others, there was the challenge and the bravado of rappelling down deep pits. Traditionally, Americans didn't view caving as seriously or as scientifically as the Europeans, particularly as the French did (the French Société de Spéléologie, dedicated to the scientific study of caves, was founded in 1895); but here, as in Europe, it attracted its share of fanatical devotion.

"In principle, caving is a lot like climbing, except it's done in the dark on rocks covered in greasy mud, and the various squeezes and crawls are so tight you end up even more cut and bruised than the average climber, which is something you simply don't notice at the time," observed travel writer Tim Cahill. "I suppose there's a bit of masochism involved, but cavers feel that the more difficult the cave, the greater the victory in having navigated it. We are people who like doing things the hard way, often for very little reward."

In their book about Kentucky's Mammoth Cave, *The Longest Cave,* authors Roger W. Brucker and Richard A. Watson noted that while a mountain climber could see his progress—where he had began and where he wanted to go—for a caver it was completely different. "Within seconds you lose sight of your starting point," they wrote. "The sinuous passages twist and turn. Always you are confined by walls, floor, and ceiling. The farthest vistas are seldom more than one hundred feet— along a passage, down a pit, up at a ceiling. You are always in a place; you never look out from a point. The route is never in view except as you can imagine it in your mind. Nothing unrolls . . . And when you reach the end, it is only another place, often a small place, barely large enough to contain your body."

But a cave, even a well-explored cave, offered something that mountain climbing rarely could—the possibility of discovering places where no one had ever ventured before. "Through even the smallest virgin passage, a caver might find marvels," Brucker and Watson wrote.

Caving could be dangerous, of course. The story of Floyd Collins, fatally pinned under a rock for sixteen days in a central Kentucky cavern, gripped the country back in the 1920s and is considered by historians to be the nation's first "media event." (Robert Penn Warren's 1959 novel, *The Cave,* was largely based on the Collins story; so was Billy Wilder's movie, *Ace in the Hole.*) But unlike many caves in the East or South, Arizona's caves were, by and large, quite accessible, often without natural barriers or deep pits. All you needed were a sturdy helmet, a pair of high boots, those three sources of light, some rope, and maybe a pair of knee pads. A change of clothes helped too, since when you emerged from a cave you were sometimes covered in mud and soaking wet, even in the drought-parched Southwest. Caving was strenuous exercise, to be sure—far more strenuous than most people realized—but to be a caver, you didn't need to be a particularly good athlete or in top physical condition; mostly, you had to be willing to slither into narrow spaces and crawl on your belly. Being small and wiry like Gary Tenen didn't hurt. At Tucson's Escabrosa Grotto, the local caving organization, you could always find two or three people willing to cave with you. And in Tucson, where there were natural marvels—both above- and below-ground—within easy driving distance, it was easy for caving to become a passion.

In the grotto, the result was a close-knit caving community, with intense and long-lasting bonds. "You were like foxhole buddies," said

Peachey. "You were put in situations where you're responsible for your partner and he's responsible for you. Teamwork is an important part. In caving, you have to go in groups of three, and you can only move as fast as the slowest of the three." And, as Peachey noted, "that responsibility toward others is often transferred to the cave itself."

With the growing national awareness about environmental matters, a sense of responsibility toward the natural world began to extend underground as well. By the 1960s, the cave organization, the National Speleological Society (NSS), of which the Tucson grotto was a branch, adopted the motto "Take nothing but pictures. Leave nothing but footprints." Some cavers became absolutely fanatical about not touching any features at all, let alone removing them. Cave formations, known collectively as speleothems (from the Greek *spelaion* "cave" and *thema* "deposit"), grow at an agonizingly slow rate, depending on place and time: a stalagmite at Moaning Cave in California has been estimated to grow an inch every four hundred years. When humans enter the picture, these speleothems can find themselves in peril. Oils from human hair and skin and lint from clothing facilitate the growth of algae and fungus, which may cause formations to lose their luster and eventually stop growing altogether.

Almost every caver had been in a cave that had been marred or destroyed by vandals, looters, or just kids out for a good time. Graffiti was rampant—Confederate soldiers scrawled their names during the Civil War on the wall at Grand Caverns in Virginia's Shenandoah Valley; so did Randy Tufts's uncle Harry Walker back in the 1940s at Onyx Cave in the Santa Rita Mountains, southeast of Tucson, much to the older caver's everlasting regret. Some visitors would take cave formations home as souvenirs, while others would remove them with the aim of selling them as bookends and ashtrays; still others just got a kick out of spray painting obscenities. At Peppersauce Cave, on the other side of Mount Lemmon from Tucson, the damage was startling: trash and graffiti everywhere, and a once-lovely cave stripped of almost all its features. In the case of Peppersauce, "A lot of the destruction happened back in the 1940s, and it extended right down to the original people who found the cave," said Tucson caver Bob Buecher. "There is actually a photo of one of the original discoverers of Peppersauce taking a stalagmite out of the cave. Things were different then. That picture appeared in *National Geographic*!" (The photograph Buecher mentions appeared in the November 1951 issue of the *National Geographic*, and a similar photo was published in the February 1948 issue of *Desert Magazine*; in captions, both magazines described the explorers posing with the stalagmite as "collectors.")

As early as 1962, after an increase in vandalism, the Central Arizona Grotto had sealed one of the two entrances at Onyx Cave and gated the other. A plaque at the entrance of what was then Arizona's most-prized cave informed visitors that a key could be obtained from the caving group. Within two months, however, the gate, made of iron set in concrete, was blown off.

Most of the caves in the West are located on public land, unlike in the East where spelunkers often have to get permission from private owners to cave on their property. Arizona cavers soon discovered that few officials at public agencies like the Bureau of Land Management and the USDA Forest Service really cared about the caves under their supervision. When Tufts and Tenen were spelunking at the Cave of the Bells in 1972, they saw a man mining the aragonite crystal for which the cave is famous and stashing it in jewelry boxes; he intended to sell it to rock shops. (Aragonite is a rare, hard form of crystal, needle-like in shape and extremely sharp, that can sometimes look like snow.) They wrote down the vandal's license number and contacted the Forest Service, which owned the property. "Did you see him remove specimens from the cave?" asked the Forest Service official. When they admitted that they hadn't, the official told them, "There is nothing we can do."

Randy Tufts poses with some of the trash he and Gary Tenen found at graffiti-scarred Peppersauce Cave north of Tucson (Gary Tenen)

Today, Cave of the Bells is an example of a cave that, in many spots, has been stripped of its formations.

In May 1974, Arizona governor Jack Williams signed into law a bill making it illegal to willfully or knowingly, "break, break-off, crack, carve, carve upon, write or otherwise mark upon, or in any manner destroy, mutilate, injure, deface, remove, displace, mar or harm any natural material found in any cave or cavern" in the state. Penalties ranged up to a $500 fine or six months in jail.

That same year, Tucson's Escabrosa Grotto made an arrangement with the private owner of Onyx Cave to lease the entrance and interior of Onyx. The grotto placed a gate on the cave entrance and offered to give the keys to anyone who wanted to cave there. The original gate, destroyed twelve years previously, had never been replaced. The gate was installed on November 12, 1974. Four days later, it disappeared. The grotto then installed a new, improved gate on November 21, and grotto members spent several days outside the cave, watching for trespassers. Two weeks later, the gate was smashed open. A third gate, put in place three days after that, was also removed, and during the following days, several people found trespassing in the cave without permits were warned and run off. On December 20, a fourth gate was installed.

"Who will win this never-ending battle?" asked the December 1974 issue of the *Desert Caver,* the quarterly publication of the Tucson grotto. "The next *Desert Caver* will contain the latest reports! In the meantime, volunteer for gate-watching duty. A successful prosecution for gate-breaking will be a fine precedent for the new cave law."

The grotto's 1974 financial statement ended with "Best Wishes to all for 1975, and kill a vandal."

It was in this atmosphere that Randy Tufts and Gary Tenen showed up at the monthly meetings of the Escabrosa Grotto, held in a downtown Tucson church. The people they met there included many who became stalwarts of Arizona and national caving over the years: Peachey; Ron Bridgemon, who later became the director of the National Speleological Society and president of the Cave Research Foundation; and Bob Buecher, an engineer who became one of the most knowledgeable people about caves in the country. Tufts's involvement in campus politics and the management of Merlin's that had limited his caving activities were winding down; by 1974 he was working as an organizer for Tucson Public Power, a community group working to oppose rate increases by the local utility company, Tucson Gas and Electric, whose rates were already among the highest in the state. Tenen was employed as a supervisor in a sheltered workshop for the handicapped and later drove a delivery truck for Hostess Cakes.

In the caving community, they were quiet and mostly kept to themselves. Known primarily for exploring Cave of the Bells, they stayed on the fringes. Other members of the grotto were aware that the two were hiking in the Whetstones; no one paid them much mind. But Tufts and Tenen had done their homework.

"The time was right, the techniques were there, it was an open field," said Peachey. "There were places where you could go without conflicts— the Whetstones were one. It was all set up for them." Randy Tufts and Gary Tenen quietly went about their business.

Exploring Xanadu

A WEEK HAD PASSED since they had found the cave in the Whetstone Mountains, and Randy Tufts and Gary Tenen had thought of little else. They returned that Saturday, as planned. For this expedition, they were better prepared, bringing two friends, both novice cavers. Things got off to a less-than-promising start when one of the neophytes, a roommate of Tufts and Tenen, proved to be too large to negotiate the tight squeeze leading into the cave; he couldn't proceed any further. Still, with the second "recruit," Eric Gill, Tufts and Tenen crawled along the rough, guano-covered cave floor and wriggled through the blowhole.

There, they split up. Tenen and Gill headed for the mud flats, the spot where the two discoverers had turned back the previous week. Tufts clambered up a pile of breakdown, rock that had fallen from the ceiling over the years. He could hear his friends' voices below. Climbing through an arched portal, Tufts immediately sensed something was different. Straight ahead loomed a black void. In the weak glow of his carbide lamp, it was difficult to grasp just how far this extended. Everything just beyond the range of his light was faint, murky, monochromatic, like a movie that suddenly switches from color to black-and-white and then fades out entirely. Tufts couldn't make out the dimensions or get any idea of walls or ceiling or floor. But, despite the darkness, he could feel the enormity of what was in front of him. The way the air moved and sounds carried indicated that he must be on some kind of overlook, and below him lay—who knew what? He called out excitedly to Tenen and Gill.

The three cavers met somewhere in the center of the vast space. Removing their flashlights from their packs, they could make out what appeared to be walls and a vaulted ceiling. They were in a large chamber that seemed to have no end: in fact, it was 400 feet long, 240 feet wide, and 50 feet high, larger than a football field. (They called it, simply, the "Big Room.") As they wandered about, shining their lights toward the fractured ceiling, the three men could see pale and delicate stalactites and soda straws dangling from jagged heights. Stalagmites, ridged and

Randy Tufts explores the muddy landscape of the Big Room (Bob Buecher)

scalloped, rose up from the floor, like pillars of some deserted temple, lost in the midst of an overgrown jungle. Crystalline shields protruded from the walls. Amidst the luxuriant beauty, there was an almost whimsical quality. The walls were decorated with thin, brownish-red, translucent sheets that bore an uncanny resemblance to strips of bacon, and there was a stalagmite that resembled a fried egg on top; the cave seemed to have a sense of humor, too. All around they could make out a veritable riot of color. The tans and browns were the result of decaying organic matter; the blues, oranges, and blacks derived from manganese; and the pervasive reddish-rust tinge caused by iron oxide.

At one moment, the chamber resembled an ancient ruined city, at another a child's fantasy garden, and, at still another, a giant cosmic joke. Like the previous week, the "tick tock" of dripping water was the only sound they heard, except for the clumping of their boots on the

Cave bacon. The striped colors are the result of the types of minerals deposited, with the red strips colored by iron oxide deposits. (K. L. Day, Arizona State Parks)

The cave's sense of humor: a formation that looks strikingly like a fried egg on a cone (Bob Buecher)

Randy Tufts's silhouette against the flowstone formations in the Big Room (Steve Holland)

rocks and their own strenuous breathing. Tufts and Tenen giggled and tugged at each other's sleeves.

No one had ever laid eyes on it before. Just looking at the sight all around them was a kind of act of creation. "I thought we were dreaming," said Tufts. "If we were to blink, it would all go away. You just realize that every gaze you cast on everything, it was the first time that thing has ever been seen. It was almost as if you are bringing it into being just by looking at it."

Meanwhile, Steve Northway, the other recruit, who hadn't been able to fit into the tight initial squeeze, had returned to the surface. As the others explored the cave, Northway sat in the sun beside the sinkhole entrance. To pass the time, he toyed with various possible names for the cave, finally settling on "Xanadu," which he took from the opening lines of the British romantic poet Samuel Taylor Coleridge's 1798 poem, "Kubla Khan":

> In Xanadu did Kubla Khan
> A stately pleasure-dome decree:
> Where Alph, the sacred river, ran
> Through caverns measureless to man
> Down to a sunless sea.

Xanadu became the name Tufts and Tenen would adopt for many years, a password to a private world of which only a tiny number of initiated knew the meaning.

After those first visits, Tufts and Tenen returned to Xanadu week after week, usually by themselves, on a few occasions with a handful of close friends or knowledgeable local cavers in whom they had confided their secret. It was essential that some other people knew where the cave was located, in case the two needed to be rescued at any point. (Gill and Northway, as novice cavers, did not participate in future trips; Northway himself gained a degree of immortality when Tufts and Tenen named

Soda straws, stalactites, and stalagmites in the Strawberry Room, named for its pink-hued formations, just off the Big Room (K. L. Day, Arizona State Parks)

the tight squeeze between the first two small rooms, "Northway's Lament," a reference to their friend's inability to make it any farther into the cave.)

Their caving expeditions mostly started the same way each time. Tufts and Tenen would leave Tucson just after breakfast for the hour or so drive in Tenen's Jeep Wagoneer, now their "official" caving vehicle. Tenen would bring a book along, usually a Rex Stout detective novel. He would prop it up on the steering wheel and read while he drove along the interstate, cruising past trucks headed across the state line to Las Cruces and El Paso. Tufts would doze in the passenger's seat, awakening with an idea that had been percolating in his mind as he slept. The two would discuss it for a while, Tufts would go back to sleep, and Tenen would return to his detective novel—and the highway.

Soon, Tufts timed his naps so perfectly that he would awaken just as the jeep was pulling off the paved two-lane highway leading to the dirt road near the cave.

As on their first visits to Xanadu, for these expeditions, Tufts and Tenen didn't take much gear, usually just hard hats, their three sources of light, some rope, a shovel with its handle shortened to fit in their packs. Tufts would bring a can of sardines, which Tenen heartily disliked because they smelled so strongly, particularly in the confined space of the cave. One food they could agree on was goosh—sweetened, condensed milk that was boiled for three hours into very portable custard. It quickly became their favorite cave delicacy. "Generally you didn't want a lot of food underground," said Tenen. "We weren't down there for a long duration. If we were in the cave for twelve to fourteen hours, we just took a couple of snacks. Caving is physical work, and you don't want to do it on a full stomach."

After caving, they'd finish the day at the Horseshoe Café, an atmospheric watering hole on the main street of nearby Benson that featured a neon horse's head on its wooden ceiling and equine murals by Western artist Vern Parker on its walls. Because it functioned as the Greyhound bus stop in Benson (population 2,839, according to the 1970 census), the place was open twenty-four hours a day and sometimes attracted a fairly rough crowd. Tenen loved the custard pie and ice cream; he'd order it every time they stopped in. Although the two would change clothes and try to clean up before arriving at the Horseshoe, it was impossible to remove all the cave mud from their bodies. Their arms and legs would remain caked with the stuff, and much of the grit found its way to the Horseshoe's floor. The restaurant's management took it all in stride. The waitresses assumed they were employed in nearby irrigation ditches—irrigation workers tended to get extremely muddy after a day's work—and Tufts and Tenen did little to disabuse them of that idea.

Randy Tufts in the remote and inaccessible Shelf Passage, discovered in 1974 (Bob Buecher)

For almost an entire year, the two men spent their weekends exploring various parts of Xanadu, corridors and small chambers and antechambers, some of them merely dark, muddy rooms filled with mounds of breakdown, others rich in ornament. They followed every lead, wriggled through every squeeze and crawlway, explored each nook and cranny as meticulously as when they had searched for holes aboveground. There were discoveries of incomparable beauty and fragility: pockets in the ceiling filled with tiny, contorted, gravity-defying helictites; rare cave pearls that were the size of marbles or pigeon eggs; a long, highly polished shelf extending from a cave wall; another wall resembling an intricately constructed maze of post office boxes. All of these deposits appeared as if they had been tenderly carved by the hand of some ancient artist or divinity; scientifically, they were the result of dripping, seeping, and flowing water that had sculpted the calcite of the limestone over thousands and thousands of years. Instead of anthropomorphic names preferred by discoverers of other caves, Tufts and Tenen gave the passages and chambers simple designations—the River Passage, the Big Room, the Cul de Sac Passage.

The cave itself was the result of geologic transformations over the earth's history. Hundreds of millions of years ago, southeast Arizona had been an inland sea. On the ancient watery floor, plants and the microscopic fragments of skeletons of marine animals compacted into

Rimstone dams with spar crystals (K. L. Day, Arizona State Parks)

a porous rock, creating limestone. The titanic force of changes in the earth's crust eventually raised up huge portions of the ocean floors, dredging up great blocks of limestone, flinging them in various directions, and producing mountains like the Whetstones. The process took millions and millions of years. Over time, groundwater seeped through the fissures in the limestone in these mountains. As the acids in groundwater attacked the calcites in limestone, underground pathways and channels formed, and as the water seeped further downward, a central channel filled up with air. Xanadu was formed in much that way, a process that culminated an estimated 200,000 years ago.

The *Myotis velifer* cave bat. Nearly a thousand roost on the Big Room ceiling from April to September each year. (Bob Buecher)

As they continued to explore, Tufts and Tenen found no indication that other humans had been there before them. The only sign of mammalian life was the maternity colony of more than a thousand *Myotis velifer* bats that roosted in the Big Room during the summer months, seeking a warm place to bear their young, and then vanished for the rest of the year. The first time that Tufts and Tenen encountered them, the two cavers were sitting and eating at an area just off the Big Room that they called the "lunch spot." Suddenly, there was a frantic squeaking over their heads—the bats were waking up. The bats made their appearance every year toward the end of April, gave birth in June, and left by mid-September. The sound of their newborns was a faint, barely audible chirping; in the dark of the cave, the mothers located their young by sound and scent.

On summer evenings, the bats used the blowhole passage as a route out of the cave in order to forage for insects, something they would do several times during the night. Tufts and Tenen would sit at the top of the sinkhole, transfixed, watching them. Tufts and Tenen's roommate Brad Barber describes leaving through the blowhole crawlway just before sunset on his first visit to Xanadu and feeling something brush against his face. When there was finally enough space above his head so he could turn and look back, he saw a line of bats coming through the crawlway at surprising speed. By the time he reached the sinkhole, "they were pouring out like a washing machine," he recalled.

Rocks with calcite coating
(K. L. Day, Arizona State
Parks)

Once Tufts and Tenen established a route inside the cave, they took
pains to stay on the trail and to avoid touching the features along the
way. They tried to step in their own footsteps, whenever possible, and to
avoid the temptation to grab on to a protruding stalagmite or stalactite
if they were about to fall.

It was the living quality that made Xanadu so distinctive, and they
were determined not to disturb it in any way. Its speleothems—the stalactites, stalagmites, and other formations—ranged in age from 40,000
to almost 200,000 years. Many of these were still growing, as water
continued to seep and flow into the cave, polishing the calcite formations, lengthening, thickening, and transforming them. The form of
these deposits generally depended on how water entered the cave and
the path the water took once inside, whether it clung to a ceiling or a
ledge (creating soda straws and stalactites), streamed down the walls
(forming flowstone), seeped out of cracks (forming shields), or dripped
onto the cave floor (creating stalagmites). If a stalactite dangled from
the ceiling, there was a very good chance that a stalagmite could be
found on the floor directly below it, created by the dripping of water
from the stalactite; with time, the two might fuse into an even more
dramatic shape, a column.

This represented a vivid contrast to Colossal Cave, which Tufts had
sneaked into as an eager teenager. Colossal is a dry and dusty cave
where the speleothems stopped growing and lost their luster years ago,

Pen and nitrocalcite
formation (Bob Buecher)

presumably as a result of drought; New Mexico's Carlsbad Caverns is
largely, although not entirely, dry as well. But Xanadu and its formations are wet, 95 percent alive. What struck Tufts and Tenen from the
moment they stepped beyond the blowhole wall was the living quality
of their discovery: the air was moving, the cave inhaling and exhaling,
the water dripping—even the mud seemed to have a throbbing, pulsat-
ing life all its own.

Overall, Xanadu proved a relatively safe cave to explore. There were no deep pits—the lowest point was only seventy-six feet below the natural entrance—and although the cave's ascents and descents required effort, they were hardly formidable, especially to experienced cavers. Unlike many other caves, Xanadu didn't require the use of harnesses and mechanical ascending equipment. The initial crawlways were extremely challenging, successfully protecting the cave from human and animal intrusion over the millennia; visitors had to crawl on their stomachs on the very rough ground, sometimes scraping ribs and ripping buttons off shirts, and then continue on their hands and knees. Deeper into the cave, the low-ceilinged crawlways were often half-filled with water; Tufts and Tenen navigated through, floating their packs ahead of them.

Early on, the two explorers discovered a one-hundred-foot-long trench that was the only route to the rear of the cave. It was filled with oozing, gurgling, primeval mud, which clung fiercely to them as they tried to make their way through it, swallowing boots and calves and making it hard to put one foot in front of the other. The mud was so difficult to slog through and so all-pervasive that it was hard to know where their bodies ended and the mud began; the mud would make their packs and their boots twice as heavy as when they started out.

"It was like walking through pancake batter or peanut butter," said Tenen. "Both layers of your pants would get covered, and your legs under the pants, too. Your boots would be covered with three-inch mud. You'd always have to bring extra clothes. You'd be soaking wet and covered with all that stuff when you got out."

Even for veteran cavers like Tufts and Tenen, there were major impediments and scary moments. Perhaps the most dangerous part began before they even got into the cave. Halfway down the sinkhole entrance was a ledge that was the residence of a local rattlesnake. The snake would usually be asleep when visitors arrived. The first person down into the sinkhole would wake up the snake—that person would make it through all right—but the second visitor could face the wrath of the rudely awakened reptile. Tenen and Tufts learned to throw stones to wake up the rattler and then wait till he departed. Tenen tended to dismiss the whole thing with a combination of modesty and bravado. "That's life in the Southwest," he'd say, but the snake's presence remained something to reckon with.

On one occasion, Tufts and Tenen decided to explore a drop in what they called the River Passage, an extremely muddy area. It looked uninviting, but they were determined to leave no avenue unexplored. The drop was about twelve to fifteen feet. Tufts remained above as Tenen, covered in mud by this point, rappelled his way down. There he found

himself in a pit that was solid rock and led nowhere. He was sure he could easily raise himself up, but because his entire body was so muddy from before he entered the pit, he had trouble ascending the rope. The two cavers didn't own any ascending gear; they couldn't afford it, for one thing. Instead, Tenen used something called a prussic knot, also common in climbing, which, when attached to the thicker main rope, formed a loop on each side into which a caver (or a climber) could insert his foot. He could move the loops gradually up the rope and ascend that way, without having to climb hand-over-hand.

But that day, as much as he tried, his hands kept slipping off the rope, throwing him back to the pit floor. Tufts was above him, joking, laughing, exhorting and encouraging him. Tenen's body felt heavier with every attempt, in part due to the mud that covered his body. The mud was very slick and greasy because of its high clay content, making the rope slick as well. He tried to remove some of the mud, first from his arms and legs, then from his hands. But, as much as he tried, he couldn't get it all off, while the rope itself was just too muddy to provide the necessary friction.

After nearly an hour, he was still at it, wondering how he had ever gotten himself in such a predicament. Then his luck began to change.

Transient pooling water amidst the pink hues of the Strawberry Room. Parts of Kartchner Caverns flood periodically, maintaining the cave's humidity. (K. L. Day, Arizona State Parks)

Gary Tenen at the Throne Room overlook (Bob Buecher)

The Kubla Khan formation in the Throne Room. This 58-foot column was created when a stalagmite, growing up from the floor, met a stalactite, growing down from the ceiling. "It's incredible and I've never seen anything like it anywhere," wrote Tufts. Note caver at bottom right of column. (K. L. Day, Arizona State Parks)

Gradually, ever so gradually, his hands began to dry off and he was able to squeeze some of the mud off the rope. Now able to get a better grip, his feet supported by the prussic loops, he made his way up the rope. Tufts grabbed his arm, and the ordeal was over. Tenen dismissed it as "a little annoyance."

On one of their earliest journeys toward the back of the cave, the two cavers stopped to enter a small room off the mud track. They turned a corner of high mud walls and came upon a dazzling white shield—five to seven feet across—that was formed by seeping water and covered with calcite; it resembled an angel's wing, they thought. The shield was all the more striking framed against the mud-brown walls. All around was a richly decorated landscape of helictites and soda straws. The Angel's Wing, as they called it, was one of the most beautiful features they had seen yet.

And then, after a year of exploration, came the most awe-inspiring sight of all. That day, Tufts and Tenen took their usual route through the mud trench, battling to stay upright the entire time, as always. But, when they came to the end of the trench, they headed down a muddy passage that they had previously, and uncharacteristically, ignored. They crawled fifty feet on their hands and knees, finding themselves in a large amphitheatre that overlooked a hundred-foot-diameter basin (they called it the "Rotunda Room"). Despite the limitations of their carbide lamps and flashlights, they could tell that they were on to something new, something that might dwarf even the Big Room.

Tufts led the way. He headed up a slope of breakdown, glimpsing a dark opening ahead in the distance. Tenen caught up with him. From the opening, they looked down upon another immense vaulted chamber, 170 feet long by 145 feet wide. In the center stood a giant column, created by the fusion of a stalactite and stalagmite—a luminous, redwood-colored, fifty-eight-foot-high, eight-foot-wide formation that resembled a totem of some ancient race. It was the height of a five-story building. They gave it the name "Kubla Khan," again after Coleridge's poem; the chamber that contained it was called the "Throne Room." Not far away was a sight almost as remarkable, a delicate 21.2-foot-long

The 21.2-foot soda straw stalactite. "Probably a record in the U.S. certainly," wrote Tufts. Soda straws grow about 1/10 inch every century, depending on the amount of water seeping into the cave. (Steve Holland)

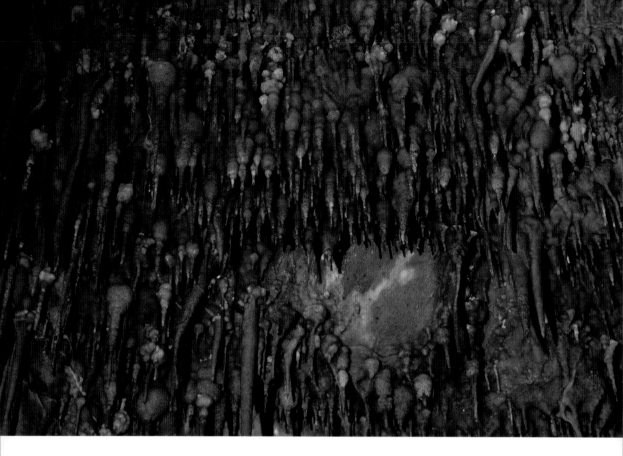

Turnip formation (Bob
Buecher)

soda straw, suspended from the ceiling. It seemed that if they breathed
nearby, it would collapse.

Once again, their expectations had been surpassed. Shortly afterwards, Tufts wrote in a letter to his uncle Harry, his mentor and guide
on his youthful caving trips, " . . . [I]n the center [of the Throne Room]
sits a 55-foot column 8 foot in diameter . . . with huge arms that pro-
trude from the sides upward. It looks like a petrified sahuaro [*sic*] cactus. It's incredible and I've never seen anything like [it] anywhere in any
pictures in any caves in any part of the country. It's completely unprec-
edented as far as my own experience goes.

"When we first came upon it . . . we just gasped. Kind of stood silent-
ly, such an awe inspiring sit [*sic*] and right next to the 55 foot column is
an 18 foot soda straw. Again probably a record within the US certainly.
We were very impressed." (Later measurements found the lengths of
both the column and the soda straw to be slightly greater than Tufts's
initial calculations.)

To Tufts, the cave was "a work of art" with "ecclesiastical" architecture. "Xanadu has the significance of an original Van Gogh or Rodin,"
he wrote later. For him, the discovery began increasingly to take on a
spiritual significance. Every time he arrived, he would bow his head
and ask the cave god for permission to enter. Then he would apologize

for any mistakes he might make in caring for it. The cave, so beautiful and remarkable, was now becoming something more—a sacred place, "holy and enchanted," as Coleridge put it in "Kubla Khan." Tufts and Tenen had been granted the rarest of privileges—and the greatest of responsibilities. How could they ever be worthy of it? And, more importantly, how could they protect it?

Playing for Time

AS THEIR ASTONISHMENT at what they had found increased with the discovery of the Throne and Rotunda rooms and Kubla Khan, so did Tufts and Tenen's concern the cave could be permanently damaged now that its sleep of 200,000 years had been interrupted. They had seen how vandals and souvenir-hunters had thoroughly trashed other caves, stripping them of formations, spray-painting walls, and dumping garbage inside. The problems that Tucson's Escabrosa Grotto was experiencing with vandals at Onyx Cave—problems which were reaching their apex at the very moment Tufts and Tenen first crawled into the blowhole passage—were very much on their minds. They worried that the same thing could happen to Xanadu. If they could find the caverns, any determined caver could do the same, especially once word got around in a community where every caver always had his or her ear to the ground for information about unknown or newly discovered caves. After all, Xanadu was located only half a mile from a major highway and only eight miles from the interstate that leads from Phoenix and Tucson east toward El Paso.

In February 1976, a year and a half after they had discovered the cave, the two men became even more concerned when they read an article in the daily *Tucson Citizen* that a "uranium rush" was starting in Arizona, with the staking of 446 mining claims in the Whetstone Mountains. It was the heyday of nuclear power in the United States—the "oil shock" of 1973 following the Yom Kippur War had dramatically raised the price of oil, and the disaster at Three Mile Island was still three years away; the demand for uranium was high. The latest claims, staked by the Kerr-McGee Company, among others, extended through fourteen miles of Coronado National Forest land, beginning six miles south of Benson and continuing southward, according to the newspaper. This would put the potential mining areas dangerously close to the cave, perhaps threatening to contaminate the waters that nourished it. "Uranium traces around the Whetstone Mountains, where there is now no mining of any type, were noted on state maps as long ago as the 1950s," the newspaper wrote, "but were bypassed by companies finding richer deposits in Colorado and Utah."

At the beginning, Tufts and Tenen had just been amateur explorers, two twenty-somethings who had discovered something amazing. Their instincts were to preserve what they had found, although they didn't know quite how. Increasingly, the thrill of discovery gave way to a realization that they had been entrusted with a profound responsibility. Xanadu was a living organism, one whose formations were still growing and changing, and, if humans didn't tamper with nature's handiwork, would continue to do so for eons more. As the two cavers saw it, their job was to keep it that way—at all costs.

"The cave had not asked to be discovered," Tufts was fond of saying. "It was minding its own business."

With an overriding sense of mission, but little idea of how to carry it out, Tufts and Tenen played for time. They decided to keep their discovery a secret, revealing it to only a handful of friends and cavers whom they absolutely trusted. Tenen didn't tell his parents, although Tufts did. In most cases, their criterion for telling someone was a "need to know" basis. They also were determined to keep it from the local caving grotto. By the mid-1970s, Tucson wasn't a small town anymore—the population had jumped from 45,000 in 1950 to 265,000 in 1970 and would continue growing at breathtaking rates. Tufts's childhood home on the east side of town, which, when he was growing up, had been just a few blocks from the desert, was now surrounded by various strip malls and shopping centers. However, the community of spelunkers was tightly knit, numbering not much more than twenty to thirty regular members. (The 1974 Escabrosa Grotto membership rolls list twenty-one members, including Gary Tenen but not Randy Tufts; membership dues were $4 a year.) And although Tufts and Tenen faded into the background of the local caving community and were known mostly for their explorations at the Cave of the Bells, grotto members were aware that they searched for caves in the Whetstones, too.

In conversation, Tufts and Tenen always referred to the cave as "X," as in Xanadu, and took pains never to utter the words "X" and "cave" in the same sentence. During their visits to Xanadu, they would cover up their spelunking implements on the seat of the car, which they parked on the dirt track that led to the cave, out of sight of the main road. In those days, the mesquite trees were less dense around Guindani Wash, just below the cave, making the whole area more exposed from the highway. When they left, they'd seal up the entrance at the bottom of the sinkhole with rocks and cover them with dust and dirt. They would put down one rock as a marker; if it was disturbed, they'd know someone had discovered their secret. The young cavers carried a

Soda straws in the Mushroom Passage (K. L. Day, Arizona State Parks)

black-and-white photo in their packs that showed the exact location of the rocks. Before they left the sinkhole, they'd poke their heads out to see if there was anyone driving or walking along the dirt road across the wash; if they noticed someone, they would go back inside until it was safe to come out. The Forest Service, which owned some of the land nearby, allowed woodcutting in the area. On one occasion, when Tufts and Tenen poked their heads out of the sink, they saw twenty or thirty people cutting mesquite with chainsaws; the cavers quickly retreated underground. If it was dark outside when they were finished caving, they blew out their lamps at the top of the sinkhole and walked to their vehicle in the dark.

When Tufts and Tenen attended those Friday night meetings of Tucson's Escabrosa Grotto, they found a very curious situation. It seemed as if hardly anyone wanted to talk to anyone else about caves, at least not in a precise way that might reveal where a cave was located. It was all couched in vague terms, if it was discussed at all. Members showed slides, but the whereabouts of a particular cave remained secret. Clean-up trips took place to Onyx Cave, which the grotto managed and which everyone knew—a test of sorts to assess the commitment of new members—and there were discussions of visits to caves out of state. But there were few, if any, organized trips to less-well-known Arizona caves. To Tufts and Tenen, concerned about keeping knowledge about Xanadu as privileged as possible, all this reticence and suspicion on the part of local cavers was actually a godsend. At these meetings, the two would hardly speak to one another. Then again, they were verbose compared to some; Bob Buecher, soon to become one of the leading cavers in the state, was particularly guarded about revealing anything and never said a word. But it all represented the culture of the Arizona caving world of the time.

For secrecy was a hallmark of Arizona cavers. The answer to the question, "Are there any caves in Arizona?" was always the laconic "None to speak of," with the emphasis on the "to speak of." This secrecy dovetailed with the cave conservation ethic promoted by the local caving grotto. The fact that most of the caves in the state were located on public land—where supervision was minimal—and were relatively accessible increased the need for secrecy as a means of protection, in the eyes of most cavers. Cavers rarely told the Bureau of Land Management or the Forest Service when they found a cave; as Tufts and Tenen discovered when they saw the man removing aragonite crystal at Cave of the Bells, those agencies were unable or unwilling to protect them.

This proved particularly frustrating for newer cavers who were eager to explore as many caves as possible but found they were not immediately welcomed by long-time grotto members. Scott Davis, who started caving in Tucson slightly later than Tufts and Tenen, describes attending grotto meetings at which "a new caver would come in and people wouldn't tell him about anything. It was a closed world and young cavers were not invited." So newcomers lingered on the fringes, hoping to pick up a bit of proprietary information here and there. "In the beginning there were three or four of us, and we were super-secretive," said Davis, referring to a group of the younger generation of cavers. "You'd discover a cave and put a trail in, using route indicators. You might come back in two years and find it trashed. And then you'd think, 'Maybe I opened my mouth up too much. Maybe I contributed to the death of this cave!'" Another approach, he noted, was "You might think, 'It's mine. I will maintain the entrance. It will remain my secret project.'" Either way, the key was not to tell anyone outside a small group of confidantes.

The secrecy was borne out by the Escabrosa Grotto's official statement of its philosophy:

The first question most people ask is "Where are the caves?" After the first question has been answered, the second question is always, "Why won't you tell me?"

Arizona cavers have been accused of maintaining an attitude of secrecy about caves. This is correct. . . .

Arizona has a problem in that several of its best caves have become quite well known to the general public. In some cases this has resulted in almost complete destruction of the cave environment . . . We do not wish other caves to take the same route to destruction. We therefore do not wish to tell everyone that beautiful, undamaged caves do exist, nor will we give precise directions to their locations since this knowledge will increase traffic in, and damage to, these caves.

However, the same document emphasizes that grotto members were willing to take novices to well-known caves, and newcomers who "maintain an interest in caving who win the confidence of other cavers" could be taken to less-well-known caves and even to relatively unknown caves in the state. But once initiated, newcomers were expected to adhere to the culture of secrecy. "By this time we would hope that their [the novices'] thoughts on conservation of caves have evolved to the point that they will not take a less-initiated group to the cave," the document concluded.

Bob Buecher argues that all this secrecy actually reflected a respect for other cavers. Everyone had his or her own secret cave somewhere, he said, so you didn't want to step on someone else's turf.

Some thought the grotto's approach was too extreme, however. The rigid emphasis on secrecy resulted in a humorous piece published in the *Desert Caver* in 1979. In "The Frustrated Caver's Guide to Finding Secret Caves in Arizona," caver Steve Holland gave some broadly tongue-in-cheek hints. Among them:

- Always wear hiking boots and a Sierra Club T-shirt . . . Never wear anything that would identify you as a caver. You must appear only as a person totally dedicated to conservation.

- Never bring up caving as a topic of conversation or you'll be labeled as a big talker.

- If invited along on a caving trip, politely refuse and explain that you feel the cave receives enough traffic already and you don't want to add to it. If you can say this seriously without cracking a smile, someone will surely be impressed.

- Attend as many grotto social functions as you possibly can. It would be favorable for you if you supplied large amounts of beer at these functions. The mouths of many grotto members increase proportionately in size with the number of beers they've had.

- Do not suggest grotto-sponsored caving trips or any trip that would be related to caving. Some good suggestions would be boulder climbing, rappelling off coaling towers, moonlight hikes, etc.
- Give wrong directions to your house. Others will be less worried about your giving cave directions to others.

Holland, who would later be a key player in a dramatic attempt to stop a group of intruders from trying to dig their way into Xanadu, summed it up this way. "There were a handful of caves in Arizona that everyone knew about," he said. "But you had to get into the loop to find out about more. You were always listening for tidbits, for pieces of intelligence." All this secrecy, he noted, "meshed well with Gary and Randy's approach."

One of the most prominent local cavers of the time was Bill Peachey, who first became involved in organized caving when he visited Onyx Cave in the mid-to-late 1960s while a student at the University of Arizona. Brilliant and gregarious, Peachey grew up in Phoenix and came to Tucson to go to college. At the UA, he was part of a group that specialized in climbing to the top of various university buildings, including the Student Union, where they placed Timex signs on the Union's clock on a number of occasions. (Sometimes, for their ascents, they dressed up in white coveralls with "Physical Plant" written on them.) Many of those involved in these pranks became the nucleus of the new generation of Arizona cavers. Peachey was also a rabid cave conservationist. Years later, he would brag about how he "took caves out of circulation" in order to save them from being ransacked and destroyed. "I make caves disappear," he said proudly. "Today you mention the names of caves that were well-known in the 1960s and nobody knows them now." In 2002, Peachey was part of a group that entered La Tetera Cave, located in Colossal Cave Mountain Park, outside of Tucson, marking the first major Arizona cave discovery of the new millennium. (La Tetera, Spanish for "teapot," was so named because it was first discovered when a passerby saw a jet of steam rising from a hole in the ground. Located on land leased from Pima County and featuring a floor covered in crystal formations, the cave remains open only to scientists.)

Not surprisingly, one of the people whom Tufts and Tenen first took to Xanadu was Peachey. The three of them talked about putting a concrete seal in the entrance of Xanadu in order to protect it. Eventually, Tufts and Tenen rejected the idea, arguing that it would actually offer a clue to someone that there might be a real cave there.

In late 1976, two years after the discovery of Xanadu and a year after they had come upon Kubla Khan, Tufts moved to Reno, Nevada, to take an eight-month job as a community organizer there, working for a grass-roots organization opposing a local utility's construction of a power plant. During this same period, Tenen rarely visited the cave. In May of the next year, Elaine Garifine, another caver whom they had let in on the secret, informed Tenen that Peachey had put a concrete seal on the cave, without the discoverers' knowledge. She herself had learned of the seal when she came upon yet another caver whom Tufts and Tenen had previously taken to the cave at the entrance to Xanadu.

Peachey had his reasons. He would later say that during this period he would go out to Xanadu to check and see if anything might be disturbed. "Essentially, Randy had disappeared, Gary, too," he insisted. He felt a "responsibility" to seal the cave. He knew that Tufts and Tenen could dig through, if they wanted.

In Tufts and Tenen's view, however, matters were clearly getting out of hand. Too many people knew about the cave, there were too many potential "loose lips," even among the small group whom they had let in on their secret. And then there was Peachey taking action on his own. "Perpetual secrecy was a chimera," as Tufts was coming to realize.

Overriding everything was the fear that Xanadu—so vulnerable in terms of location, so easy to explore once you got through the initial crawlways—might be prone to re-discovery and potential destruction.

Around this time, Tufts and Tenen read a series of articles by Russell H. Gurnee and others, originally published in the quarterly *Bulletin of the National Speleological Society,* called "Conservation through Commercialization." In an article on the Rio Camuy Cave project in Puerto Rico, Gurnee advocated "controlled protection" of a cave by turning it into a tour cave—the kind of development that "will provide protection for this natural resource [Rio Camuy] as well as enjoyment and education for millions of people in this and coming generations."

It was a seemingly counter-intuitive notion: that the most effective way to save an untouched and pristine cave was to develop it as a tourist attraction, a "tour" or "show" cave. Yet, the more they thought about it, the more the idea made sense to Tufts and Tenen. That way, at least, no one would be able to strip the stalagmites and soda straws, spray-paint the shields and flowstone, and generally wreck havoc in their Xanadu. In fact, some of the vulnerabilities of the cave in terms of fending off vandals—its closeness to a main highway, proximity to Tucson, and relative shallowness—could actually be turned into assets for develop-

ing a show cave. Many other show caves were in relatively obscure locations, far from large cities and airports. Carlsbad Caverns in the remote southeast of New Mexico, the Caverns of Sonora in West Texas, even Mammoth Cave in central Kentucky were examples of this, to varying degrees. By comparison, Xanadu's location was almost ideal.

Creating a tour cave had its drawbacks, to be sure, but keeping it a secret and hoping for the best had drawbacks, too, even if word never got out. The fate of a nineteenth-century Cobleskill, New York, farmer named Lester Howe hovered in the background. The story goes that Howe began to notice that whenever it was a hot day, his cattle kept returning to the same mysteriously cool spot on a neighbor's land. The spot turned out to be the entrance to what would later be called Howe Caverns. He bought the cave from his neighbor in 1843 for $100 and turned it into a successful tourist attraction, the third show cave in the United States (after Mammoth Cave in Kentucky and Grand Caverns in Virginia). But he overextended himself financially, building a hotel at the entrance and a miniature railroad inside the cave. After losing the cave to his creditors, Howe found an even more spectacular and beautiful cave that he named the Garden of Eden. But he refused to tell anyone where it was—he had suffered a financial setback in the cave business once before, after all—and eventually died without revealing his secret. To this day, Howe's "Garden of Eden" has never been found.

Even if Tufts and Tenen and their small circle of confidantes successfully kept their cave secret for years and years, could it meet the same fate, disappearing into the mists of time and history? Bill Peachey might have preferred that course; Tufts and Tenen weren't so sure. The idea of protecting Xanadu while sharing it at the same time increasingly attracted them.

So, in the summer of 1977, Tufts spent two months hitchhiking across the country to visit some other caves and to see how Xanadu compared, if it was as magnificent as the two friends believed. At a time when hitchhiking was more commonplace and acceptable than it is today, Tufts thumbed rides with a sign that read "Anywhere but Here." And hitchhiking was full of adventures. "Hitching per se has been very enjoyable, offering a twinge of excitement each morning I go out," he

Stalactites
(Steve Holland)

wrote his roommates Gary Tenen and Brad Barber in a long letter from Thetford Center, Vermont, dated August 20 of that year. "Staying in one place for any length of time is the oddity. You know the exhilaration you feel the morning of a trip—it's almost each day for me. And getting into a car is like stepping into a theater in the middle of a movie. Everything is absolutely unpredictable. From the rides you get to the places you crash."

By that point in his trip, he had visited Lehman Caves at Great Basin National Park in Nevada, Wind Cave National Park in South Dakota, and Howe Caverns in upstate New York. "Xanadu is definitely as intriguing as those—it's a better cave in many respects," he wrote. "I'll know more after I visit Luray [caverns in Virginia] and Mammoth [cave in Kentucky]."

The glories of Luray, one of the oldest and most beautiful show caves in the country, and the vastness of Mammoth, the world's longest cave, didn't dissuade Tufts. He decided to move back to Tucson from Reno, taking a job in his hometown as local coordinator for the Neighborhood Reinvestment Corporation, a Washington, D.C.–based non-profit that organized housing programs and partnerships around the country. In his spare time, he would work with Tenen on developing the cave. The first thing they had to do was to get access once again. By moving some rocks around, they were able to bypass Peachey's concrete plug, creating an alternative route into the cave proper.

Then they got to work. Their goal was to see Xanadu protected as a tour cave, while at the same time avoiding the hokeyness associated with such enterprises. "Our intent also is to make this a very educational cave," Tufts wrote to his uncle Harry. " . . . in other words one that has good scientific explanations, not merely the slipshod explanations of formations that you hear in many caves, that have good dioramas and displays outside. My geological background can help with that. We want it of course to be a healthy experience for people, so they are not endangered by going on tour. We want it to be a good all-around attraction which makes us some money and at the same time is not a ticky-tacky operation."

As would become their approach throughout the next decade, they methodically began to research all aspects of the venture. The two caving partners established a joint bank account under the name "Double T Enterprises" (for Tufts and Tenen) and attended a Chamber of Commerce session entitled, "How to Start Your Own Business." They had long-distance telephone conversations with the executive director of the National Caves Association (NCA), the grouping of cave owners and operators. And they made the first tentative steps toward raising money. Tufts approached people he knew, including his uncle Harry.

Randy Tufts in the Angel's Wing area. "Xanadu is as intriguing as those [some early caves he visited]—it's a better cave in many respects," he wrote. The formation looks like an angel's wing or a frozen waterfall and results from minerals deposited by flowing water. (Gary Tenen)

Through all this, Tufts and Tenen were developing their own working relationship. Both were very methodical and detail-oriented, and they would sit and brainstorm to what sometimes seemed the point of absurdity. "We spent ten times the amount of hours planning and thinking than we spent in the cave," Tenen said. "For big clumps of time we weren't caving at all, just talking. Both of us were really contemplative. But Randy's bent was toward analysis-paralysis; my bent was toward impulsiveness." Often, Tenen would stop analyzing an issue or problem or scenario earlier than Tufts, finally enabling things to move ahead. And when Tenen wanted to do something rash, Tufts was there to put the brakes on. "I would get us off the spot when we couldn't make a decision, and there were times that Randy would hold me back from doing something we shouldn't," said Tenen. "It was highly collaborative and that is what made us a great team." He added, "If it was left to Randy, we'd still be thinking about it. If it was left to me, it would not have been as well thought-out."

Yet there remained a major hurdle—to approach the owner of the land. At first, the two young cave discoverers had assumed that Xanadu lay on Forest Service or Bureau of Land Management property. They soon found out that that wasn't the case. In fact, the land was owned by James A. Kartchner, of St. David, a small town several miles from the cave. However, just because they had discovered something under Mr. Kartchner's land didn't give them any legal rights to it. Their plans and dreams would somehow have to involve Mr. Kartchner.

But who was the Kartchner family? Tufts and Tenen spent six months researching the Kartchners, digging through deeds and records and accounts of local history. A friend of Tufts who worked for the *Tucson Citizen* pulled every article from the newspaper's archives that had any reference to the family. The two cavers talked to people who knew the Kartchners by reputation—or knew people who knew them—so the family wouldn't know they were investigating them. "We analyzed everything that we did," Tenen said. "We'd spend hours talking about the 'what ifs.'"

Toward the end of 1977, Tufts and Tenen approached Mr. Kartchner indirectly, through a real estate agent. The agent drove to St. David and found the civic-minded Mr. Kartchner up on a ladder in front of the town post office, shingling the roof. Would he be interested in selling any of his land in the Whetstones the agent asked him, as off-handedly as possible. No, Mr. Kartchner replied, the land had been in the family for a long time and he didn't believe in selling land, anyway.

Had he indicated any interest, as it was Tufts and Tenen didn't have the money. In part they were just trying to assess the situation, to get a sense of his attitudes. If Mr. Kartchner had been willing to sell to someone who approached them as casually as their real estate agent, that might mean that if they told him there was a cave on his property, he might sell to the highest bidder. In a way, his "no" was reassuring.

But as time passed, it became clear they could wait no longer. If any of their ideas were to come to fruition, they would have to speak to Mr. Kartchner directly.

JAMES A. KARTCHNER purchased the eleven-square-mile property in the foothills of the Whetstone Mountains, at the outlet of Middle Canyon, seven miles over dirt roads from his St. David home, in 1941. He had always dreamed of being a rancher and had originally bought the property for raising livestock; at one point one hundred head of cattle grazed on what the family called the Lower Section of the Whetstone Ranch. During the war, his two oldest sons, the twins Mark and Max, would spend weekends at the ranch, keeping an eye on the horses and camping out in abandoned ranch houses. On one occasion, they had climbed through a wash of mesquite trees and come upon the Xanadu sinkhole—Max even lowered himself part way down—but were scared off by a rattlesnake.

Mr. Kartchner himself may have suspected something strange as he stood on top of the two limestone hills on the northwest section of his property from which he could watch his livestock grazing on the flat land below. He and his sons would ride down the hills on horseback, the hoofbeats echoing like a drum. "You know, it sounds like these hills are hollow," he told them.

When the two cave explorers finally decided to approach Mr. Kartchner themselves, Tufts telephoned and told him simply, "We found something on your land that we think you should know about." Tufts still didn't mention the word "cave" or describe exactly what property he was referring to. Mr. Kartchner said he'd be happy to meet them in person.

So, late in the afternoon on Monday, February 20, 1978, Gary Tenen and Randy Tufts left Tucson in Tufts's Rambler for the hour-and-a-quarter drive to the old Mormon settlement of St. David. The two cavers traveled along the interstate east toward Benson, the lonesome ranching town that also served as the location of their favorite after-cave watering hole, the Horseshoe Café. It was beginning to get dark and just a little cold by now; in southern Arizona in winter, the sun goes down early and quickly, and the temperature drops precipitously

SIX

Encountering the Kartchners

as well. On the backseat of the car lay a borrowed slide projector and a carousel with images of Xanadu. Tenen had also brought along slides he had taken of Peppersauce Cave near Tucson, whose once-stunning formations had been totally stripped and that now was a trash heap of broken beer bottles and graffiti-scarred walls. (One slide they didn't include was one of a naked woman that had been spray-painted on the Peppersauce wall; they were concerned the Kartchners might be offended.) Along with the slides, they also brought some old photos of how Peppersauce originally looked before the looting and desecration. It was from that fate that they were determined to save Mr. Kartchner's cave, if only he would let them.

During their months of research on the Kartchner family, they discovered that in addition to being a rancher, Mr. Kartchner was a retired teacher who had been the superintendent of schools in St. David. He and his wife Lois were the parents of twelve children, six of whom were medical doctors. Mr. Kartchner had been born in Utah, of Mormon pioneer stock, and had come to Arizona in 1929 during the Great Depression to teach vocational agriculture and mathematics at Benson High School. Lois Kartchner had been born in northern Mexico in one of the Mormon colonies established there in the 1880s. The couple met when she came to Benson to attend school. In 1938, Mr. Kartchner accepted the position of superintendent of schools at St. David, the next town down the road south of Benson, a job he kept until he retired in 1971.

Tufts and Tenen had quickly decided that an understanding of the family's Mormonism was absolutely crucial to developing any relationship with them. Before they approached the family, they busied themselves reading works on the history, religion, and culture of the Latter-day Saints. "We interviewed Mormons, we interviewed people who knew Mormons, we read almost every book we could get our hands on," said Tenen. "We discovered there were over 4,800 members of the Kartchner clan." They also talked to an anthropologist who had done his dissertation on the Latter-day Saints and who cautioned them that, in dealing with Mormon pioneer families like the Kartchners, they could face a "development-oriented," anti-environmental point of view and a wariness toward outsiders.

It was a potentially awkward encounter—Tucson's Vietnam War-era counterculture meets small-town Mormon pioneers—and Tufts and Tenen wanted to be as prepared as possible. If anything, they had over-prepared. They spent hours writing down every potential scenario on yellow notepads and composing an elaborate script for the meeting. In fact, they had done so much research that Tenen was getting frustrated. He wanted to make sure the Kartchners were on board as soon

James A. and Lois Kartchner. "We were pretty sure they would be honest, salt-of-the-earth type of people," said Tenen. (Dean Kartchner)

as possible. Temperamentally, though, neither one could be anything but methodical.

There were grounds for optimism. From everything Tufts and Tenen had heard and read about them, the Kartchners were clearly an educated, even outstanding, family, people who might share their goals. For one thing, Mr. and Mrs. Kartchner were extremely public-spirited, involved in all sorts of community activities in St. David. Mrs. Kartchner had been named the Mormon church's "Arizona Mother of the Year" in the late 1960s, and Mr. and Mrs. Kartchner had won the Joseph Smith Family Living award from Brigham Young University. It was said that Mr. Kartchner had initiated science courses at the St. David High School so his sons would know enough science that they could eventually go to medical school. (Mark and Max, the oldest sons, graduated from medical school at Harvard and Cornell respectively, unusual for a small-town Arizona family of relatively modest means.)

"From our research, we were pretty sure they would be honest, salt-of-the-earth type of people, straightforward," said Tenen. "They didn't seem the type of people who would turn stalagmites into bookends and ashtrays."

Despite the encouraging signs, the two cavers were very concerned about making the proper impression. Tenen shed his usual army-surplus garb for a pressed shirt and khakis and trimmed his beard, making him look less like a Latin American revolutionary and more like the sort of polite young man who might ask someone's daughter to a college dance. Soon, he would shave his beard for a five-year period in order "to be cleaned up to develop a relationship with the Kartchners," as he put it. The usually clean-cut Tufts didn't have to effect such a transformation.

Still, the whole project could definitely fall apart. Who knew how the Kartchners might react? What was to say that Mr. Kartchner wouldn't just thank his visitors for the information and then dismiss them and tell them to stay away from his land? Although the two cavers hadn't trespassed on Kartchner property, according to the legal definition of the term, would Mr. Kartchner be annoyed that they had waited so long to tell him? "Here we are going to tell them about it [the cave]," Tenen recalled. "What are they going to do with it? Well, they could develop it themselves. They could keep it a secret and we would work with them. They could dump us. They could throw us out on our ear. Would they just turn around and advertise the fact that there was a great cave and sell it?"

Perhaps Tufts and Tenen might have taken into account the fate of the Campbell brothers, the discoverers of Luray Caverns, the beautiful show cave in Virginia's Shenandoah Valley, back in 1878. After finding the caverns, the Campbells had kept it a secret, buying the land where Luray was located for $13 at a bankruptcy sale. When the original owners found out about the existence of a cave on their former property, they went to court, claiming they had been cheated; the judge gave the owners their land back. The two situations were not precisely analogous, of course, but what was clear was that a discoverer of a cave on someone else's property didn't possess much in the way of rights.

St. David was a town of fewer than 1,500 souls, strewn along a highway just south of Benson, dominated by the church of the Latter-day Saints and the high school. It lacked the orderly, grid-like town planning that characterized many Mormon towns in the West, although there were still examples of graceful Lombardy poplars, the trademark of Mormon settlement, along the main road. Mr. Kartchner came out to the front of the house to greet them. He and his wife lived in a modest clapboard bungalow, and their visitors found it hard to imagine that the couple had raised twelve children in so small a space. Then seventy-eight, Mr. Kartchner was a fine-looking man, weathered, wiry, and still quite fit. Mrs. Kartchner was the model of the country wife, with just a hint of steeliness behind her eyeglasses; she spent most of her time knitting, crocheting, and keeping track of her many grandchildren's birthdays. A fire was going in the living room, and photos of three generations of Kartchners stared down from the mantelpiece.

There was a bit of stiffness and formality on both sides, and the two cavers proceeded cautiously, at first without mentioning the word "cave." "If anything comes of what we're going to talk to you about, we'd like to be treated fairly," they said. Mr. Kartchner replied, "I've always treated everyone fairly." Tufts and Tenen asked to be included in anything that might result from what they would tell him, and Mr. Kartchner agreed. Finally, the two young men described Xanadu, how breathtaking it was, how well it measured up against the top tour caves in the country. "Oh, over in that property near the Whetstones," said Mr. Kartchner matter-of-factly. "We once found brachiopod fossils there." Tufts was slightly relieved—obviously Mr. Kartchner's knowledge of science extended beyond high school textbooks.

The lights were dimmed, and the visitors set up their slide display of Xanadu and the vandalized Peppersauce Cave. Tufts did most of the talking—he was the persuasive one, schooled in diplomacy, the college politician after all, who had bested President Schaefer in so many campus battles. As images of extraordinary cave formations danced before their eyes, there were no "oohs" and "ahs" from the Kartchners, just respectful attention. Tufts and Tenen weren't sure what to make of their reactions, but they pressed on valiantly in the dark, just as they had on that first day at Xanadu. The two sides were cautiously feeling each other out. The Kartchners "were people of few words," said Tenen. "Quiet is their way."

When Tufts broached the idea of developing Xanadu as a tour cave, Mr. Kartchner gave some inkling of what was going through his mind. "You could get a lot of people through there," he replied. There were chuckles all around.

As the lights came back on, Tufts returned to his main point. "Our only request," he said, "is that whatever you decide to do with this, we'd like be involved."

Mr. Kartchner nodded approvingly.

The tension had lifted, and by the end of that evening, a sense of trust seemed to be emerging on both sides. "The Kartchners were absolute people of their word," says Tenen. From the family's point of view, the third oldest son, Dean Kartchner, put it this way: "They got along very well. There was no question in my parents' eyes as to how Gary and Randy stood."

Mr. Kartchner indicated that he would like to go and see the cave and bring his sons with him. And so it was set.

After their visitors left, the parents had a talk with Shella, their youngest child who was in high school and still living at home. "Don't you say anything about this," her father told her firmly.

Following their visit, Tufts and Tenen wrote the Kartchners two letters. In the first, dated March 8, two and a half weeks after their meeting, the two cavers emphasized what they hoped would be their own participation in any decisions the Kartchners took regarding the future of the cave. "As we had agreed, the first priority is to build a working relationship that includes all of us," they wrote. "As the cave's discoverers, we feel responsible to steward it. Prudence dictates that no actions be taken without careful study and that we keep in mind the cave's delicacy and continuing vulnerability." They ended on a note of optimism: "We were excited that you shared our appreciation for the cave and grateful that you are willing to include us in plans that might be made."

The second letter, dated April 26, was more practical in nature, offering some advice on the family's upcoming trip to the cave. "Because Xanadu is a live, active cave, be prepared to get wet and muddy," the two cavers wrote. "Also it will be necessary to crawl for short distances through tight, tube-like passages where your clothes might be torn . . . Wear sturdy boots providing some ankle support because the floor is rocky and slippery in places . . . We will provide the needed hard hats and lights although each person should bring a small flashlight as a backup. Each person also should bring a small lunch, such as a sandwich, nuts or a candy bar, packed in a crush-proof plastic container."

A few days later, Tufts and Tenen met the family at the cave site. It was a warm spring morning, and the foothills of the Whetstones were coming alive. The mesquite trees along the wash that ran at the bottom of the hill near the sinkhole were in leaf; red blossoms were in such profusion that they bent the arms of the tentacle-like ocotillo that covered the rocky hills. Suddenly, an entire group of Kartchners appeared out of nowhere, "as if they lived intimately among the rocks and trees of the site," in Tufts's view. On hand was the patriarch himself and five of his sons—Max, Dean, Paul, Fred, and Glen. It was the first time that the sons had met Tufts and Tenen. The two cave discoverers, both of whom had grown up in small families, were amazed at how many of them there were; they joked that they would need nametags to keep track.

On this occasion, although some of the awkwardness and reserve of that first meeting with the parents remained, everyone was clearly excited. Max Kartchner, an anesthesiologist, brought a camera with him. Almost as soon as he entered the cave, he began taking one flash picture after the next. Tufts and Tenen were afraid that Max would run out of film before he reached the Big Room. "Save your film!" Tenen told him—the best was still to come. None of the Kartchners had ever been caving before, much less with a couple of strangers. Mark Kartchner, Max's twin, was at work, performing surgery, and Mrs. Kartchner was not with the party; she never saw the cave until years later.

Wearing yellow hard hats with carbide lanterns and sporting denim shirts and jeans, the group let themselves down into the sinkhole. Once they had navigated the first few rooms and arrived at the cramped, low-ceilinged crawlway that led to the blowhole, Tufts pulled aside the two youngest brothers, Paul and Fred, "both lean and skinny as rails," as their older brothers described them. "We want you guys to go through first because we think if you can make it then everyone else will come," Tufts told them. "But we think you can make it a little easier." The brothers were a little surprised. The initial rooms hadn't been a problem at all; they didn't expect that the crawlway would be any different.

Tenen led the way, and Paul and Fred followed, slithering forward on their stomachs. They made it easily. But then it was Dean's turn. Dean was huskier than his brothers, and as soon he began to maneuver himself through the crawlway that led to the blowhole, he realized he was in trouble. "You really had to be a contortionist to get through that crawlway," he said. "You really couldn't see ahead." As he struggled, he heard his brother Fred, in front of him, call out, "This really gets tight!" "That's when my heart sank," Dean said. "I thought maybe someone could pull my legs from behind, if they had to. But I was really worried."

He was having trouble going forward, but he knew he couldn't go backwards. The buttons on his shirt had popped; he could feel skin tearing on his back. Dean, who was in his early 40s, was the third oldest brother, an anesthesiologist who shared a medical partnership with two of his brothers and lived outside of Benson. He and his wife had thirteen children. He was easy-going, slow-talking, devout. Later in life, when the kids were grown, he and his wife would go on adult missions to Colombia and Chile. But that day he wasn't feeling very adventuresome. "I'm never coming back here again," Dean promised himself.

Finally, Dean made it to the blowhole. He exhaled to try to make his size smaller. He put one arm forward and the other arm down along his leg, as Tufts instructed. He contorted his body in every way possible. But, no matter how hard he tried, he couldn't get through that hole. Then Tenen, who was already on the other side of the opening, and Tufts, who was behind Dean, came to the rescue. As Dean lay in front of the blowhole opening, the whole party waited as the two experienced cavers produced hammer and chisel. For half an hour, they attacked the hard limestone, opening up the hole just enough so Dean could get through. Finally he did, feeling exhausted and frazzled. "We made the opening Dean-sized," Tenen said jokingly. The rest of the family followed through without incident, including Mr. Kartchner.

And then, quickly, they found themselves at a point where they could stand up. Dean saw stalagmites rising from the floor and sta-

"Tough as nails": James A. Kartchner, age 78, crawls through the blowhole (Dean Kartchner)

lactites and groups of soda straws just above his head, and the same streams of bright orange flowstone that Tufts and Tenen had encountered on their first visit. Everything seemed to shimmer; he was thrilled by the tiny drops of water glistening at the ends of the stalactites and soda straws.

Tufts and Tenen had originally been most concerned about Mr. Kartchner, but he seemed completely unaffected by the rigors of the ordeal. "Mr. Kartchner was of pioneer stock and he was tough as nails," said Tenen. "At that point, to trek through the cave was really a lot of work. I remember that Mr. Kartchner wore boots but no socks. Nobody ate or drank the whole way underground. But Mr. Kartchner seemed fine. Here was a man who was on horseback every day of his life. Nothing seemed to bother him."

That day, they visited only the Big Room and other areas toward the front of the cave. To get to the Rotunda Room and the Throne Room, with its 58-foot-high Kubla Khan column, required swimming through high water and battling the mud trench. Tufts and Tenen calculated it would be too much for the Kartchners, given Mr. Kartchner's age and the family's lack of caving experience. That expedition would have to wait for another trip.

On the first visit though, the family was awestruck. What they saw was utterly beautiful and inspiring, and it had been sitting under a piece of land they had taken for granted for so many years. Suddenly, they viewed the world—their world, their property after all—in a completely new way. At one point, through the cave ceiling in the Big Room, they could actually see the roots of a mesquite tree that stood on the hill

Mud flats area (K.L. Day, Arizona State Parks)

The Kartchners stop for a photo next to some large stalagmites toward the end of their first trip to the cave. From left, Max, Fred, Glen, Dean, Paul, and James A. Kartchner. (Gary Tenen)

James A. Kartchner (left) and son Fred (Gary Tenen and Kartchner family)

A new partnership: from left, Milo and Dwight Kartchner, sons of Dean; Dean Kartchner (front); Gary Tenen (rear); Randy Tufts (center); Kevin Kartchner, son of Mark (front in yellow helmet); James A. Kartchner; and Fred Kartchner (Kartchner family)

above them; they were just a few feet from the outside where they had played as boys and rode horses when they were older. Family members saw the hand of God at work. "When Dad was telling me about it, I thought, sure, probably a little hollow in the hill," said Max. "And so when I went in I was astounded. . . . I really had the sense that here was almost something divine, more like a cathedral or temple. That it was just a work of deity and something that was God-given and certainly had to be one of the beauties of nature."

After more than four hours, they slowly made their way back, in a state of exhaustion and exhilaration. The party stopped in front of a cluster of towering stalagmites for a photograph, looking somewhat dazed but content. And as much as all of them dreaded having to re-negotiate the blowhole passage and the crawlway in order to get out, the return was without problems.

Once they were outdoors, the weather had shifted dramatically. It had been warm outside before the group entered the cave, but by the time they made it back, it was a chilly forty degrees with a biting wind; a cold front had blown through and the temperature had dropped twenty degrees within minutes. But that didn't matter. There was still another part of the initiation rite to undergo: the consumption of Mrs. Kartchner's fresh lemonade, sitting in jugs next to their vehicles, amidst the flowering ocotillo and scraggly cacti. "Drink it, drink it!" Mr. Kart-chner entreated everyone—his wife wouldn't let him come home with that lemonade unfinished. Mr. Kartchner, who had refused every offer of water during the entire time they had spent inside the cave, was extremely thirsty himself, consuming what seemed like almost a gallon of the stuff. "It was freezing outside and we were all soaking wet," said Tenen. "But we had to drink Mrs. Kartchner's lemonade—all of it. That was courtesy. And the lemonade was ice cold, too."

Afterwards, the Kartchner sons went back to Dean's house to hose off the mud and change clothes. The consensus of the brothers was that "it was great that we had the opportunity, it was a superb experience, but never again," said Paul Kartchner, twenty-eight, the ninth oldest of the family. "The only thing that was bad was the crawlway and the blowhole and everything else was not a problem. But everyone said over and over again: 'Great. A superb experience. But never again!'"

Those vows didn't last long, however. That was particularly the case with Dean who, despite his difficulties that day, became perhaps the most enthusiastic of the brothers about the exploration of the cave. Meanwhile, the day's events—capped by the communal drinking of the lemonade from plastic cups—seemed to seal the arrangement between Tufts and Tenen and the Kartchner family. As they left, Mr. Kartch-ner asked Tufts and Tenen to prepare a proposal. They were going to be partners now, with the great work of cave stewardship and development still ahead. Soon, Tenen would quit his job as a driver for Hostess Cakes to work full-time on the cave. Soon, too, the Kartchner family would lock the gate to the property to keep away intruders. Soon, it wouldn't be Xanadu anymore; although no one knew the name yet or even conceived of the possibility, it was beginning to be Kartchner Caverns.

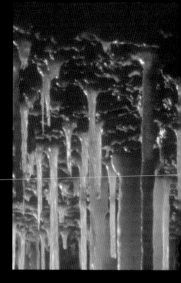

PART TWO

The Making of Kartchner Caverns

IT WAS AROUND THIS TIME that Gary Tenen and Randy Tufts became Lewis and Clark. They needed to make phone calls, write letters, approach strangers, and pay for various expenses—all just to explore the possibility of making Xanadu into some sort of commercial (or perhaps non-commercial) venture. The two cavers feared that if they used their real names, they were apt to be found out and the truth of what was lying under the Kartchner property would come to light. Tenen took the name Mike Lewis; Tufts was Bob Clark. They printed up business cards with their new names. Tenen insists to this day that the choice of the pseudonyms "Lewis and Clark" was inadvertent; they only realized the significance later. But, in retrospect, it was appropriate: like the two explorers who mapped America in the first decade of the nineteenth century, in their own modest way, Tufts and Tenen had discovered a new world.

SEVEN

Lewis and Clark in Tucson

BOB CLARK

2810 E. SYLVIA
TUCSON, ARIZONA 85715   (602)297-3215

Randy Tufts's "Bob Clark" business card (Gary Tenen)

In keeping with the approach of secrecy, they paid for everything involving the cave in cash, wary that signing checks might give away their identity. They used the Los Angeles law office of Tenen's half-brother's brother (who had a different last name) as their mailing address. The Kartchner family knew them as Tufts and Tenen, of course. But when Orion and Jan Knox, cave cartographers from Texas, came to map Xanadu, Tufts and Tenen only revealed their real names over dinner at a Tucson restaurant and only after the Knoxes had signed a secrecy agreement. When Tenen attended a National Caves Association (NCA) conference at Lake Shasta Caverns, California, he did so as Mike Lewis. Meanwhile, their attorney drafted a legally binding secrecy document, which the two men insisted that everyone they told about the cave had to sign.

In the fall of 1977, Gary Tenen met a young woman named Judy Quinlan. Attractive, self-confident, with an entrepreneurial bent, she was a former schoolteacher who owned a Baskin and Robbins ice cream franchise in Tucson. Gary, who was still working for Hostess Cakes during this period, dropped by the shop at the suggestion of a mutual friend. The two went out on a date to "Tucson Meet Yourself," an annual festival, created by UA folklorist "Big Jim" Griffith, that celebrates the city's cultural diversity with everything from old-time Western swing music to Tohono O'odham native circle dances. The two hit it off, even though Gary fell asleep with his head on the table when they went out for coffee afterwards, according to Judy's account.

Then, on their second date, matters turned more serious. Gary arrived at Judy's northwest Tucson home, carrying a sheaf of papers under his arm. "If I am going to continue to see you, I need you to read this contract and sign it," he informed her.

They sat in her kitchen and she went through the contract. It read: "Please sign this letter to indicate your understanding that any information you receive relating to a cave known to us as Xanadu located in Cochise County, Arizona, is being imparted or gained by you pursuant to a relationship of special trust with the undersigned and associates. The existence, location, description, and all other aspects of Xanadu, as well as any of your observation or activities connected therewith, constitutes proprietary information with monetary value of at least several hundred thousand dollars . . . Your signature to this letter represents your promise that you will not reveal any information about the cave without the permission of the undersigned and will not use any such information for your own advantage."

Judy was mystified. It was only the second time they'd gone out and already she had a legally binding contract in front of her. "I had no idea what it was," she recalled. "I didn't know Gary was a caver. I knew nothing." Still, after glancing through it, she decided the document seemed "pretty innocuous." She signed. "I don't know what would have happened if I hadn't signed!" she said. Then, Gary proceeded to let her in on the secret of the cave, taking her there for the first time a few months later. They married in July 1979.

For Judy, it sometimes seemed like she had married a secret agent. "We would go to Escabrosa Grotto meetings and Gary would never say anything," Judy said. "We would be places and I'd ask him a question.

And he would look around furtively to make sure there was no one in the restaurant who could potentially be a caver."

Then there was the incident, unrelated to secrecy, that occurred early in their marriage after Gary went caving at Xanadu during a particularly wet period. His clothes were covered with mud—the mud at Xanadu had "a lot of clay in it, and it was a fine, very silky mud that would completely saturate," Judy noted—and the couple didn't have a washing machine at home. So they drove down to the local Laundromat and put Gary's wash in the machine; as his clothes spun around in the Speed Queen, they bore an uncanny resemblance to chocolate pudding. The attendant kept frowning in their direction. After a while, he came over and told them, "We don't allow dyeing here!" and insisted that they leave. Judy couldn't believe that she was actually being kicked out of a Laundromat. Then again, it wasn't totally unreasonable. "If you opened the lid, there was this brown, frothy stuff," Judy said. "You would take wet clothes out of the washer to take to the dryer and it would just be brown muck, dripping across the Laundromat floor."

Judy did tell some members of her family about the cave, with Gary's permission. By the time of their marriage, her mother and father and one brother knew. Her sister in Tucson and her brother in Yuma still hadn't been told, nor had her other siblings back East. "My sister in Tucson was talkative and didn't need to know, and because she lived in Tucson, she was the one who could put the cave most at risk," Judy noted.

At first, Judy believed that Gary and Randy were being somewhat paranoid in all their emphasis on secrecy. "I thought it was weird," she said. "Absolutely. What was the big deal?" But then Gary sat her down in front of the same slide show of Peppersauce Cave that he and Randy had shown to the Kartchners that first meeting; he also brought her to some caves where little of the original ornamentation remained. Some years before, as a school teacher, Judy had taken a class to Peppersauce, which was "wiped pretty clean" by that point. "You catch on pretty quickly," she said.

The Kartchner family soon became practiced in the arts of secrecy as well. It was a rite of passage for the family's younger generation to be told the secret of the cave and taken on a group trip to the caverns, led by the discoverers. (By 1980, the twelve children of James and Lois Kartchner had seventy children of their own, and the grandparents had nineteen great-grandchildren.) This usually occurred when they were about to enter high school. "We wanted to make sure they were old enough so they could be relied upon not to tell anyone," said Dean Kartchner. Kathy Kartchner, daughter of Dean's brother Mark, remembers her first trip to the cave this way: "You had to change your clothes right there, so no one would know. Telling anyone was a cardinal sin." Potential spouses of Kartchner family members were not informed about the cave until the marriages took place. The family kept photograph albums of family visits to the cave hidden and separate from other photo albums. And a large, framed color photo of the Kubla Khan formation, presented to Mrs. Kartchner by her children, remained out of public view on her bedroom wall.

Tenen argues that all this insistence on secrecy was not exaggerated on their parts. "We were crazy, but we felt it was better to err on the side of overkill than not," he said. "We really wanted to protect the cave beyond our lifetimes. It was like having kids—it changes your life—and the cave was like our child. We would do anything to protect it."

In October 1978, Tufts and Tenen presented their proposal to the Kartchner family. A thirty-two-page document, with notes, bibliography, and appendices, it took them six months to complete. The two cavers were living next door to one another at the time and were constantly revising it, delivering new drafts and corrections, arguing passionately, and staying up late. They would write out drafts in longhand on legal pads, cutting and pasting sentences and paragraphs from previous drafts into what increasingly resembled a jigsaw puzzle. One room in Tenen's house was covered with butcher paper on which they scrawled brainstorming ideas in colored marker. A former roommate who was an English Ph.D. candidate edited the final draft. Tufts's girlfriend, Sheri Livney, who had agreed to type the proposal, was increasingly frustrated over all the changes. For the two cave discoverers, the document "represented our trial by fire in terms of commitment," said Tufts.

The proposal was extensively researched, in the usual Tufts-Tenen manner, with chapters on the science of caves, on some of the problems caves faced (such as overuse and vandalism), and on the history of their exploration of Xanadu (called "X" throughout). "We suspected the Kartchners didn't know much about caves," Tufts noted. "So we deliberately included a portion that included background on caves. We wanted them to have a clear perspective on caving as a sport and caving in Arizona and, in particular, the problem of vandalism. We wanted them to understand that cavers can be fanatics and that the passive forms of protection that we had been utilizing up to that point were unlikely to be successful."

The explorers listed four options for preserving Xanadu: gating the entrance; sealing the cave; opening it as a research center; and commercializing the cave. The document carefully laid out the drawbacks of the first three. Entrance gates "signaled the existence of a cave" and were "notoriously prone to forced entry," as the Tucson grotto had learned at Onyx Cave and other cavers had learned repeatedly across the coun-

Randy Tufts surrounded by butcher paper on which the two cavers scrawled brainstorming ideas (Gary Tenen)

try. Sealing would create "a false sense of security"; wouldn't prevent prospecting, drilling, or mining which could damage the cave; and, at the same time, would allow "no utilization of those features of the cave which give it value [meaning the scientific, educational, and aesthetic]." At the same time, "X" probably wasn't large enough in area and didn't have the diversity of cave life to justify its establishment as a research facility. And after the research ended, "the inevitable notoriety and publicity the cave will have received will only magnify the protection problem," they argued.

That left the fourth remaining option, commercialization. Admittedly, they had visited many caves which were "over-commercialized and reflect[ed] a tourist-trap mentality," Tufts and Tenen wrote. But in recent years, they noted, several cavers had become cave developers or managers, demonstrating "that it is possible to commercialize a cave tastefully and present it to the public educationally, factually, and profitably." The Caverns of Sonora in West Texas provided their model for a tasteful, educational cave that had been privately developed. So, they gave commercialization their "preliminary" approval, concluding, "Unlike the other options discussed, commercialization provides an opportunity to realize X's scientific, educational and economic potential and, at the same time, protect a valuable resource."

When Tufts and Tenen went to St. David to present the document to Mr. Kartchner, they found that the Kartchners had already come to the identical conclusion on their own. The family had already decided "to go with your program," as Mr. Kartchner put it, giving the two cavers its blessing to begin investigating the idea in more detail. It would be a collaborative venture. The family had already locked the gate to its land—to the dismay of many of their neighbors for whom it was the only natural passage to the Middle Canyon area of the Whetstone Mountains. Along with Tufts and Tenen, the Kartchners opened a joint bank account, the "Cochise Explorers," to fund expenses in connection with the project. The two cavers agreed to contribute half the money and the Kartchners the other half. The first use of funds sent Tenen to the NCA conference, where he made valuable contacts with cave owners, managers, and experts who would play influential early roles at Xanadu.

It was after that conference that Orion Knox and his wife Jan came on the scene. Orion Knox, who lived in Austin, Texas, had a reputation as one of the best cave cartographers in the business; in 1960, as a college student, he had been one of the discoverers of a cave, Natural Bridge, near San Antonio, Texas, which he had helped to develop and turn into a tour cave four years later. Tenen called him on the phone—or rather, Mike Lewis did. "I want to talk to you about mapping a cave," he said. "Where is it?" Knox inquired. "Somewhere west of the Mississippi," replied Mike Lewis. Knox was somewhat bemused by this. When, after much back and forth, the cave mapper was close to agreeing to take the job, he tried to catch his caller off-guard. "What airport will I be coming into?" he asked. Mike Lewis's reply was: "It's in Arizona." That at least was a little more precise than "somewhere west of the Mississippi." All this changed once the Knoxes arrived in Tucson, however, and Mike Lewis metamorphosed into Gary Tenen.

The Knoxes spent four and a half days at Xanadu in mid-December 1978, along with Tenen. Tufts, who was working full-time at his Neighborhood Investment Corporation job, had met the Knoxes the evening they arrived but was unable to be present for their cave visit. The group stayed in Benson at the San Pedro Motel, next door to the Horseshoe

Dear *Orion Knox* :

Please sign this letter to indicate your understanding that any information you receive relating to a cave known to us as Xanadu located in Cochise County, Arizona, is being imparted to or gained by you pursuant to a relationship of special trust with the undersigned and associates.

The existence, location, description and all other aspects of Xanadu, as well as any of your observations or activities connected therewith constitutes proprietary information with monetary value of at least several hundred thousand dollars, which information belongs exclusively to the undersigned and his associates, including the owners of the cave. Unauthorized disclosure of such information or its personal use by you in any manner would be a breach of this agreement giving rise to damages.

Your signature to this letter represents your promise that you will not reveal any information about the cave without the permission of the undersigned and will not use any such information for your own advantage.

Very truly yours,

Gary Tenen

UNDERSTOOD AND AGREED: *Orion Knox*

Early version of secrecy agreement that Tufts and Tenen required all Xanadu visitors to agree to and sign. Here it is signed by cave mapper Orion Knox. (Gary Tenen)

Café, where they would return each evening covered with mud and grime; it was the kind of place where no one ever came in to change the sheets though, and by the time they left, their rooms were filled with the dust of dried mud, and the shower stalls had mud splattered all over them. Roy Davis, a cave entrepreneur who had developed Cumberland Caverns in Tennessee and who Tenen had met at the Lake Shasta NCA conference, joined them; his role was to assess whether "X" had any real potential for development.

When Davis arrived a couple of days into the mapping, he found Orion Knox extremely enthusiastic. "Roy, the cave is terrific, another Natural Bridge," Knox told him. But Davis, whose visit to the cave got off to a difficult start when he had trouble navigating the initial crawl-way, was more cautious. The Big Room, the first large chamber, didn't seem that striking to him. He was impressed by the helictites and soda straws around the Angel's Wing, the white shield just off the Subway Passage, leading towards the back section of the cave. But it was when he continued on the muddy trek to the Rotunda and Throne rooms that he totally changed his mind. The 21.2-foot soda straw in the Throne Room was, in his view, "the one we all dream of." His final evaluation, announced over drinks at the Horseshoe Café: "It deserves first-class treatment."

Meanwhile, Tenen was impressed by Orion Knox's cave-mapping techniques. "The guy crawls through the cave using his elbows, and his hands stay perfectly clean so he can map and sketch," he said. "This guy can go through a small crawlway, three-quarters filled with water, and keep his hands clean and his notebook dry." The result was a map of a large portion of the cave that showed nine thousand feet of passage, more than the discoverers had originally assumed; it also showed the Throne Room to be located directly underneath the highest hilltop visible from the sinkhole entrance. After Knox left, Tufts and Tenen continued mapping the rest of the cave over a six-month period, a sometimes arduous process that featured moments such as Tufts standing waist-deep in water in a passageway behind the very long soda straw, holding the measuring tape out to Tenen who was standing up to his armpits in water in the same passage. But Knox had offered the first accurate and professional mapping of Xanadu, giving the place a more solid kind of reality than it had ever had before. It was literally on the map—somebody's map, anyway.

In January 1979, shortly after the Knoxes' visit, Tenen, using his pseudonym, arrived at the Caverns of Sonora in West Texas. He spent two months working there, learning how to construct trails and excavate tunnels, and then journeyed east to spend two months at Luray Caverns in Virginia's Shenandoah Valley, helping to install a new light-

ing system. He was determined to learn the cave business from the ground—or more accurately, underground—up.

Gary Tenen in deep water in the Rotunda Room during flooding (Bob Buecher)

The Caverns of Sonora, located midway between Austin and El Paso, were first opened in 1960 and are considered by many cavers to be the loveliest in the United States; its trail system was being extended at the time Tenen arrived. Jack Burch, who had leased the cave from its owners back in 1959 and had done the original engineering of trails, stairs, and handrails, was in charge of the new project. At Sonora, Tenen learned how to wield a heavy rock drill and gained experience in the use of dynamite to blast for trails and tunnels. He and the rest of the crew of four, including Burch, would spend a portion of the day drilling holes in the rock and a portion of the day building plywood and two-by-four baffles to protect the cave from the effects of dynamite. Then came the blast, and the crew would follow up by "mucking out the muck" with a wheelbarrow. "I got the biggest set of blisters I've ever had in my entire life," Tenen said. "It was incredibly hard work with the humidity and the heat and the heavy rock drill and the dust and the noise. You get in the best shape you've ever been in. It's like doing jackhammering in a sauna."

Sonora is a cave filled with delicate formations—it is famous for its exquisite butterfly-shaped helictites—and the passages are narrow, many of them covered in a carpet of crystals. There, Tenen learned that it was possible to develop a cave with minimal damage as the work proceeded. He also learned what not to do. According to Tenen, Jack Burch would decide what formations would stay and which wouldn't, as if he were some minor cave deity. "In walking through the new trail before the tourists got there, Jack identified the formations that he was going to pluck," said Tenen. "I thought it was sad. He kept a light attitude about it but he'd walk through, pretending he was a tourist—'Those get plucked, those get plucked!'" Burch has been quoted as saying—with not a little hyperbole—that more delicate formations had to be destroyed during the original development of Sonora than were known in all the world's other caves.

At Sonora, there had been a moment that demonstrated some of the perils of working under a false identity. Because of its reputation, the Caverns of Sonora was a major gathering place for cavers from all over the country. Sure enough, two weeks after Tenen/Lewis departed, another caver from Tucson showed up there. "We just had someone from Tucson working here for a few months," the manager of the caverns told him, explaining that his visitor had a specific interest in learning about trail construction. "What was his name?" the visiting caver asked. "Mike Lewis," replied the manager. The visitor was puzzled. He was sure that he knew every caver in Tucson—it was a small community, after all—but had never heard of anyone by that name. The visitor was Bill Peachey, one of the first people whom Tufts and Tenen had taken to Xanadu.

By this time, Tenen was at Virginia's Luray Caverns, learning to install lights and working with Roy Davis, the entrepreneur who had come out to Xanadu with the Knoxes. Davis's approach was to conceal lights so no bulb or fixture or wire was visible at any point on the trail. That could be a particular challenge at the points where there were forks in trails or trails that ran near each other. Tenen learned these skills and again got a glimpse of what he and Tufts hoped to avoid at Xanadu: in Tenen's view, Luray lacked a "conservation ethic," was over-commercialized—a glimpse of silent-film idol Rudolph Valentino's Rolls-Royce was included in the cave admission price—and even possessed the world's largest pipe organ, which played "Oh Shenandoah" and almost twenty other tunes, using the resonance of stalagmite formations.

At Luray, as at the Caverns of Sonora, Tenen worked undercover. Although Roy Davis knew him as Gary Tenen, everyone else at Luray believed his name was Mike Lewis. He checked into a hotel as Mike Lewis, his co-workers called him Mike, and even Davis would address him as Mike. Using a false name, especially while traveling, soon became second-nature to Tenen. "People don't realize the name you've given them is an alias, of course," he said. "So if someone called out 'Mike' and I hesitated for a moment, they would assume I was daydreaming, not that Mike wasn't my real name."

Pseudonyms, however, were difficult to maintain when both Tufts and Tenen were together. At a cave seminar they later attended in Missouri, they instinctively called each other by their real names, rapidly destroying their cover. Adopting names other than their own also proved a double-edged sword. Over time, various cave experts learned they were using pseudonyms, resulting in some raised eyebrows. "According to Roy Davis, some people would have been more willing to give us far more information, had they believed we were dealing straight with them," said Tufts. "They simply didn't appreciate the situation. Those that did, understood why we were going to such great lengths. I must admit it was rather Byzantine, however."

Learning to run a tour cave went beyond the development process, requiring more than proficiency at trail construction and lighting. It also involved understanding the financial aspects of the operation— what made a tour cave profitable? how should it be managed? who would come? So Tenen wrote a series of letters to various cave owners whom he had met at the NCA conference, trying to get some insight into the business side. In a letter to Gary Roberson of Marengo Cave in Marengo, Indiana, dated October 13, 1979, Tenen starts off with his usual air of mystery: "As you know I am involved in a project to develop a cave in the Southwest." Then he requests various data: What is the annual number of visitors? How far away are you from the nearest metropolitan area? Percentage-wise where do your visitors come from? How close are you to an interstate highway? What would you estimate as your penetration of the market? What is the walking distance of your tour and how long does it take? In terms of finances, he wanted to know: What was the relationship between admissions, gift sales, and other income productions? What is the breakdown by percentage of gross revenue of expense items such as utilities, advertising, payroll, rent, repairs, taxes, etc., etc.? The letter is signed Mike Lewis; the return address is that of Tenen's half-brother's brother, Norm Goldenberg, in Los Angeles.

From all the evidence—Tenen's travels, his talks and correspondence with cave owners and operators—the development of Xanadu looked like it would be difficult and relatively expensive, and they would have only one shot. But Tenen became convinced it could be done. "All of us agreed that we wanted to turn it into a private, non-profit corporation like the Arizona-Sonora Desert Museum [the world-renowned zoo and natural history museum on the outskirts of Tucson]," said Tenen. He added, "We were afraid of having the state or federal government take it over because of the public process involved in any kind of acquisition.

If the government agreed to acquire it and then if the appropriation was delayed or didn't happen, how could the cave be protected? We were concerned that, during the process, word would get out and the place would be destroyed."

Adding to Tufts and Tenen's sense of optimism was their relationship with the Kartchners, who were increasingly coming to see the cave as a family treasure. A year after the first Kartchner visit, the two cavers took Mr. Kartchner and several of the sons on a muddy trip to the farther section of the cave that the Kartchners hadn't explored previously, featuring views of the Angel's Wing shield and the Rotunda and Throne rooms, including Kubla Khan. That was followed by visits by even larger groups of Kartchner family members, guided by Tufts and Tenen and culminating in feasts of Baskin and Robbins ice cream at the cave site, courtesy of ice-cream entrepreneur Judy Tenen. The vows that the Kartchner sons took after that first trip about "never again" crawling through the blowhole proved short-lived. They embraced the cave enthusiastically.

After those first two visits, the cave "became a part of living" for the family, said Max Kartchner. "Every four to six months, we'd sign off and get lost for a Saturday. They were always willing to take us on another trip in."

Despite the many cultural differences between them—for example, Randy didn't have any children, while Dean had thirteen and Max eight—those trips truly cemented the relationship between the discoverers and the family. Dean, who had had so much trouble getting into the blowhole that first time, would watch the bats exit the sinkhole on summer evenings and was involved in extensive mapping of the cave with his children as the years went on; he even discovered a passage overlooking the Big Room that Tufts and Tenen had never seen. Tufts and Tenen developed great respect for the Kartchner clan, viewing it as a "superior species," in Tufts's words, people who were disciplined, followed directions, and could always be relied upon. Years later, Tufts would remind Paul Kartchner how remarkable his family was, telling the story of addressing a group of schoolchildren at a Benson school and asking the principal if there were any Kartchner children in that group. And the principal replied, "Yes, there are two or three of them and they raise the IQ by 20 points." That became one of Tufts's favorite stories.

For their part, Mr. and Mrs. Kartchner invited Tufts and Tenen to their fiftieth anniversary party, held outdoors in June 1980 at the St. David school. With a couple of hundred people in attendance and hordes of children and grandchildren running around, the Kartchner sons barbecued a cow that they had slaughtered for dinner, and after-

A family treasure: a muddy Dean Kartchner (right) and his children emerge from a visit to the cave (Gary Tenen)

wards everyone played softball. "It was a classic trip back to Americana of the '40s and '50s," said Tenen. Still, it was a bit awkward; Tufts and Tenen couldn't tell strangers exactly how they knew Mr. and Mrs. Kartchner and the family.

The bond Tufts and Tenen established with the parents had extended to the children almost right from the beginning. "Within Mormon culture, the authority of the father is absolute," Tenen noted. "Once the father said we'd be treated fairly and included, the kids followed what he said." But the relationship took on a life of its own. Over the years, Tufts and Tenen would hold late-night confabs with some of the Kartchner sons in the back corridors of St. Joseph's Hospital in Tucson, where they worked as doctors. (Max, Dean, and Paul were anesthesiologists, while Mark was a surgeon.) And when Tenen suffered a ruptured appendix, it was Mark Kartchner who would perform the surgery.

"For me, there were two discoveries in the course of this project," Tufts observed. "One was the cave itself in all its wonder; the other was the Kartchner family who became such good friends." Referring to Tufts and Tenen, Max Kartchner said, "We planned together, we lived together, we shared together. My feeling is that Gary is just another brother."

Despite all the memorable journeys underground and despite Tufts's and Tenen's extensive research on tour caves, this period of optimism did not last more than a couple of years. The Kartchners were beginning to have doubts about the feasibility of developing Xanadu as a commercial venture. It was 1980 and the United States was immersed in the Iranian hostage crisis, the cost of gasoline had skyrocketed again, the economy was sputtering. The "malaise" that President Jimmy Carter had identified in his famous television address the year before was trickling down even to a tight-knit, small-town clan like the Kartchners. Around this time, Mr. Kartchner and two of his sons took a week-long cruise from Vancouver through the Inner Passage of Alaska sponsored by Howard Ruff, the celebrated investment adviser who, in his spare time, sung solos with the Mormon Tabernacle Choir. Ruff's book *How to Prosper during the Coming Bad Years,* published in 1978, topped the *New York Times* bestseller list for two years running, and his monthly publication *Ruff Times* was the largest financial advisory newsletter in the world. It was an "educational cruise," featuring six-hour-long daily instruction in finances, investments, and the like. Ruff's central philosophy was one of fiscal caution: his book offered advice on how to protect yourself financially by investing in gold, silver, Swiss francs, real estate, and various other hedges against the inflation that was rampant in the 1970s. He strongly discouraged anything that smacked of risk. After one of the cruise seminars, amidst the clouds and mist of the fjords of the Inner Passage, the Kartchners cornered the great man himself and asked him point-blank about developing the cave. Ruff didn't hesitate to voice his opinion. "Just forget it," he said.

When the Kartchners returned, they told Tufts and Tenen that it didn't make economic sense to try to develop the cave on their own. The two discoverers were stunned. Their own research had appeared so promising; the figure they had come up with to develop the Big Room—$354,000—was high but certainly not impossible to achieve. But their advice paled next to that of the investment guru; they had no choice but to go along with the Kartchners.

Then, things worsened. On a mapping expedition in May 1980, Tufts and Tenen discovered that someone had been getting into the cave.

Not just "another pretty cave": Tufts at the Cul de Sac Passage (Gary Tenen)

THE MAKING OF KARTCHNER CAVERNS

Their rock blockade had been moved, and although the intruders had done a careful job of putting it back in place when they left, Tufts and Tenen could still tell someone had been there, perhaps more than once. There weren't any signs of vandalism inside, just one broken formation, which appeared to be an accident. That convinced them that the intruders were most likely cavers, not looters. But who? They obviously couldn't go around and ask at a grotto meeting without blowing their own carefully constructed cover. The two discoverers considered camping out at the cave site for three weeks and waiting, something neither had the time or the desire to do. Finally, they installed a gate at the bottom of the sinkhole along with a warning notice stating that the cave was being supervised and studied and that trespassers would be prosecuted. They deliberately made sure the gate was not impregnable; their fear was that if it was too strong, the intruders might start digging somewhere else on the hillside, causing additional notice.

Tufts was in Salt Lake City on a business trip when the phone rang at 2 a.m. in his hotel room. Only one person would call at this hour—Gary Tenen. And sure enough, Tenen's voice was on the other end of the scratchy connection. "We found out who it was!" he announced excitedly. "One of them is dating Kathy Kartchner, Mark's daughter. She had nothing to do with it. It was a chance connection."

Kathy Kartchner was a freshman at the University of Arizona and a member of the university women's gymnastics team. She herself had been to Xanadu on two occasions, introduced to it for the first time, like so many of her generation of Kartchners, when she was in high school. Many of her college friends were involved in "extreme sports"—skydiving, scuba diving, and spelunking. One Friday afternoon, she was sitting around at a UA student hangout with some of these friends, including her boyfriend at the time. They started to tell Kathy how they had been to a cave, moved some rocks aside, and crawled in on their bellies. They talked about bringing her boyfriend along the next time; he hadn't been there yet. The more her friends described the cave, alarm bells began to go off in Kathy's head. When she asked where the cave was and one of her friends replied, "Over by Benson," there was no longer any doubt in her mind. It *had* to be the same place. "You're not supposed to be doing this!" she shouted. Kathy quickly alerted her cousin—her college roommate and the daughter of her uncle Max Kartchner—who told Uncle Max who then told Gary Tenen.

The intruders turned out to be active members of the Tucson caving community, all nineteen, twenty, and twenty-one years old, and they were soon the recipients of a late-night visit from Tenen. One of them was Scott Davis, as gung-ho a caver as any in the grotto. Tenen told them point-blank, "We know you guys are getting into our cave."

Tenen demanded that they sign a secrecy agreement, but they would have nothing of it. He also offered the opportunity for them to return to the cave whenever they wanted, but only if accompanied by himself or Tufts; they declined to take him up on that either. Still, Tenen's visit had the desired effect. "We gave him our word though and never went back after that," Davis said.

Davis claims that he and his friends were just checking out Xanadu—which they knew as Crackerjack or "CJ," the name given to the cave by the two cavers, John Porter and Lane Larson, who had explored the sinkhole and the first two rooms in the spring of 1971 before Tufts and Tenen discovered the cave. It was just one on a list of "wild," undeveloped caves Davis and his friends explored. "We were all over the state," he said. "Caving was our passion." They got into Xanadu four or five times, he admitted, arriving there at dark and parking two to three miles down the road and up a dirt track so no one would see them. To Davis, Xanadu was "just another pretty cave. There were others just as pretty." After talking to Tenen, though, they decided it wasn't worth pursuing. "We were busy caving elsewhere and realized this was a sensitive cave, so why bother?"

Clearly, to Randy Tufts and Gary Tenen, Xanadu was not just "another pretty cave." It was far more important than that. The situation with Scott Davis and his friends had been cleared up, to the discoverers' great relief. But with the Kartchners' withdrawal, Xanadu was suddenly and unexpectedly in a state of limbo.

The Years in the Wilderness

IT WAS A DECEMBER DAY in 1984 when Randy Tufts drove up to Phoenix to talk to Arizona State Parks. State Parks, which owns and manages scenic and recreational areas and historical monuments throughout Arizona, was a small, mostly neglected agency in those days, but Tufts was taking no chances. He knew that state government didn't exactly have a reputation for being close-mouthed; everything tended to leak in Phoenix. So, shortly after he walked into the office of Charles R. Eatherly, the State Parks official in charge of scouting new sites, Tufts asked if he could shut the door. Eatherly was surprised; practically the only time anyone shut the door at the State Parks offices was when personnel matters were the topic of conversation.

For Tufts and Tenen, not much had changed in the three and a half years since the Kartchners had decided to withdraw from developing Xanadu. The cave had been their passion, the center of their lives through the 1970s. But once the Kartchners had taken Howard Ruff's advice and determined that now was not the time for a risky financial venture, the two cavers' hopes had been dashed. For a while, they tried other avenues. Tenen approached a member of the board of directors of Tucson's Arizona-Sonora Desert Museum, asking if the museum might ever be interested in taking over "something of high caliber worth protecting," a sort of "Desert Museum east." Tenen's language was deliberately vague—he never used the word "cave"—and the board member indicated that that was not the kind of thing the museum would ever consider. Tufts and Tenen also approached a representative from the National Park Service, who was noncommittal. The group trips with the Kartchners to the cave continued; so did the underground mapping with the help of Dean Kartchner and his sons. The dream was alive, but the prospects for the future appeared bleak.

It was a time of anguish, and opportunity, for the two longtime friends. They didn't know what their next move should be, as far as Xanadu was concerned. At the same time, other aspects of their lives were taking center stage. Gary Tenen had a growing family to support.

He and his wife Judy had started their own business, a franchise of the national chain AlphaGraphics that specializes in printing for business needs. Soon, their three Tucson locations were the highest-volume franchises in the AlphaGraphics system. They were rapidly becoming successful businesspeople. Their first child, David, was born in 1982, followed two years later by a daughter Julia, and by a son Levi in 1989. Tenen was the one who took the Kartchner family on a number of trips to the cave during this period. He served as the "quartermaster" for these operations, keeping a supply closet in his house crammed with an array of hard hats and carbide lamps and packs.

Meanwhile, Tufts had moved to Denver, where the Neighborhood Reinvestment Corporation had established a regional field office. From there, he made frequent visits to revitalization programs he pioneered in cities such as Los Angeles, San Diego, Houston, and Casper, Wyoming. In many respects, he was happy to be away from Tucson. As he wrote in one of his journals, "I feel not trapped, enmeshed in a web of memories, old friends, etc. and much freer in Denver." Perhaps, in a way, he was happy to be free of Xanadu as well.

Tufts kept extensive journals, as was his habit throughout most of his life. There was hardly a passing thought or an idea that didn't find its way into one of his spiral notebooks. He was still dreaming big dreams, even if they didn't revolve around Xanadu. His Gatsby-like 1981 "Master Dream List" included the following: to take a trip around the world; to be an astronaut; to be very well read; to be outgoing and personable. In his notebook jottings during this period, he tried to analyze his own interest in caves, recalling his childhood love for the book *Five Boys in a Cave* and his high school expeditions to Colossal and other caves. "The discovery of the cave [Xanadu] by others led me to fear for its safety and jolted me into a mood to act," he wrote. "I also was so proud of it that I wanted to share it."

As Tenen was settling down to put down roots and raise a family, Tufts was restless. He had had a number of serious relationships with women but seemed unwilling to make the ultimate commitment. On New Year's 1984—the time of the year when he would annually review his life and where it was heading—Tufts decided to quit his job and fulfill his dream of traveling around the world. But moving on wasn't that simple: he stayed in Denver for the most of the year, finally leaving his position at the Neighborhood Reinvestment Corporation in October 1984. That same month, he spent three weeks with a group of strangers on an Outward Bound trip in the spectacular Canyonlands National Park of southeastern Utah. The trip would be a rigorous, challenging experience, a course in outdoor activity that "promised extremes of heat and cold, sore muscles, bad food, little sleep, general unpleasantness," as he wrote in an account of the trip, completed soon after he returned home. The three weeks included carrying sixty- to-seventy-pound packs on grueling hikes and culminated in a marathon. (Tufts had taken up running seriously during his Denver years, participating in the Denver Mayor's Cup Marathon and other races.) In the evenings, the group leader would read the poems of Robert W. Service, the poet known as the "Canadian Kipling" for his ballads of the turn-of-the-century Yukon Gold Rush. Service's poem "The Quitter" quickly became, for Tufts, the anthem for the entire experience:

> When you're lost in the Wild, and you're scared as a child,
> And Death looks you bang in the eye,
> And you're sore as a boil, it's according to Hoyle
> To cock your revolver and . . . die.
> But the Code of a Man says: "Fight all you can,"
> And self-dissolution is barred.
> In hunger and woe, oh, it's so easy to blow . . .
> It's the hell-served-for-breakfast that's hard.

As Tufts wrote in his account of the trip, "There were many times when I felt like stopping or slowing or going back or not getting up but always found some way to persist . . . Whenever I took the opportunity to assert myself, project my own personality, 'let my light shine,' it was worth the price of admission . . . Whatever my attitude, I willed it in one way or another . . . It was up to me and always has been."

The whole period could be characterized as an early version of midlife crisis—Tufts had just turned thirty-six in August of that year. The motivation for the proposed round-the-world trip, in his mother's view, was an effort "to find himself." Part of the purpose, too, was to gain some time and distance in order to think about the cave, specifically to decide how much of a role he wanted to play in its future, if any. But a trip around the world had been the number one heading on his "Master Dream List," and that in itself may have been the central underlying reason.

Before he left on his travels, Tufts made a trip to Tucson to visit friends and family. Not surprisingly, once back in Arizona, the cave beckoned. He paid a call to Ed McCullough, who had been his geology professor and college adviser and was now the dean of the faculty of science at the University of Arizona. As he was driving to McCullough's office, he realized that it was the tenth anniversary to the month of their discovery of Xanadu. Tufts's mind was racing; by the time he arrived, the cave was suddenly in the forefront of his thoughts again. Was there was any possibility that the UA might be interested in using Xanadu as a research site, he inquired of McCullough, even though he had dismissed that very notion in his and Tenen's original proposal to the Kartchners years before.

McCullough had a better idea. He called Tufts's attention to a recent report that had revealed that Arizona ranked forty-ninth out of the fifty states in terms of the number of state parks. Only tiny Delaware had fewer. Arizona had only twenty-one state parks as opposed to New Mexico's thirty-nine and Utah's forty-six, spending a pathetic $1.11 per person per year to operate them. Part of the reason was because there were so many national parks in Arizona and so much federal land, many Arizonans didn't even think the state needed a state parks system; the State Parks agency itself was only established in the late 1950s. The state's young governor, Bruce Babbitt, who had been elected in 1978, wanted to change all that. In his view, Arizona State Parks was "a very sleepy place," focusing more on recreational facilities, like boat slips, rather than on the state's natural wonders; he was determined to invigorate and expand it. He also had national political ambitions, which wouldn't be hurt by a revitalized park system. Under Babbitt's prodding, State Parks had acquired a number of sites, including Catalina State Park near Tucson (which had impressed the Kartchners); Red Rock and Slide Rock parks outside of Sedona; and the Homolovi Pueblo Indian ruins near Winslow. McCullough suggested that Tufts talk to the people at the State Parks agency.

Tufts conferred with Tenen and the Kartchners. Usually he and Tenen made decisions in a slow, careful manner. But on this occasion— perhaps reflecting the despair that had gripped them over the past three and a half years—they moved swiftly. They decided to approach Arizona State Parks.

So on that December day, instead of seeing the sights of Bangkok or Bombay as had been his original plan, Tufts found himself in Charles Eatherly's office in Phoenix. During the two-hour drive up from Tucson, he worried anew that getting state government involved might jeopardize the secret of the cave. Eatherly, a tall, angular Texan with a laid-back manner and a pronounced drawl, was a State Parks veteran. He had been working at the agency since 1971 in a variety of capacities, primarily dealing with land and legal issues; previously he had worked in park-related jobs in Texas, Oklahoma, and Arkansas. His official title was special projects coordinator. Sitting in Eatherly's office, Tufts asked Eatherly to give him some idea of the state's procedures for park development. But when Eatherly asked, "What kind of

resource are we talking about?" Tufts replied, "I can't tell you." Eatherly
followed up by asking where this mysterious resource was located, and
once again Tufts answered, "I can't tell you." They talked some more
about the steps that the agency was required to follow in the acquisition of property for a park—first it had to be approved by the Arizona
State Parks Board, then it needed to go through the legislature, Eatherly
explained. The whole process would take two years at an absolute minimum, if they were lucky.

According to Eatherly's account, as the conversation progressed,
Tufts was still unwilling to utter the word "cave," and Eatherly had no
suspicions. But there was something about Tufts's presentation that
piqued the State Parks official's interest. "I didn't know who he was but
just the way he talked about it, you could feel his excitement," Eatherly
said. "There was a kind of electricity when he spoke."

Tufts asked Eatherly if he would be willing to come out to the site.
"This is something you must see!" he told him.

So the following month, in January 1985, Eatherly met Tufts and
Tenen at the San Pedro Motel in Benson. Eatherly says that he still had
no idea what he had come to Benson to look at. Tufts had suggested
that they meet in late afternoon. Eatherly thought this was strange—he
figured they would leave in the morning, take a hike, go look at this
property, whatever it was. Tufts had informed him that his friend Gary
Tenen would come along. The three went to dinner at the Horseshoe

Café, where Eatherly noticed Tufts and Tenen were talking in "hushed tones," almost in whispers. Toward the end of the meal they told Eatherly, "We are going to the site tonight." Eatherly replied that would be fine, thinking "maybe it is one of those stargazing places."

Eatherly recalls the evening vividly: they returned to the motel and then, when they got into the car, Eatherly says, Tufts and Tenen asked if he would object if they blindfolded him. Things were getting even stranger, but the affable Eatherly agreed. One of them took out a bandana and covered Eatherly's eyes. They drove around Benson in various directions so that their visitor would have no idea of what route they were actually taking. Eatherly couldn't help but think back to his days as an undergraduate at Texas Tech when he was pledging a fraternity; he and the other pledges had been blindfolded and taken "out into the country" for a kind of a hazing ritual. "I really wasn't concerned," he said of that drive with Tufts and Tenen. "I thought it was really strange. I've been in a lot of situations like this and didn't feel it was dangerous." When they told him, "We're going to meet family members," Eatherly felt reassured. But he still had no idea what was at the end of the journey.

After a while, they slowed down and went through a gate, and the road became extremely rough. A few minutes later, they stopped the car. Tufts and Tenen removed Eatherly's blindfold and introduced him to members of the Kartchner family. Four brothers were present.

The group took a walk around the property. It was a beautifully clear evening, Eatherly remembers, with no moon, and the sky was suffused with stars. It might well have been one of those "stargazing places." The first clue of what was in store came when Tufts said, "We are going to go underground. It doesn't matter whether it is night or day. It is dark in there all the time." For the first time, Eatherly realized that what he had come to see was actually a cave. Soon, they were at the edge of the sinkhole, and everyone was outfitted with hard hats and flashlights. "You'll just have to drop over the edge here," Tufts and Tenen told him. Eatherly looked in that direction; it was a twelve- to fifteen-foot drop and he wondered how he was going to get back out.

Eatherly lowered himself into the sinkhole and didn't have much difficulty making it through the initial dusty rooms. But when he reached the beginning of the tight crawlway that led to the blowhole, he began to have trouble. At 6'3", he was taller than Tufts or Tenen or the Kartchners. His chest was thicker in those days, and he got stuck. He couldn't move forward or back; the rocks on the floor of the passage and those on the ceiling seemed to be rubbing on his front and his back. He turned pale and began to sweat profusely. It became evident to everyone that Eatherly was not going to make it any farther. Finally, the State Parks

Strawberry Room with "Strawberry Sundae" at left (K. L. Day, Arizona State Parks)

official was able to disentangle himself, and they all sat in one of the small rooms near the sinkhole and chatted until Eatherly managed to stop sweating. There, on the cave floor, the cave discoverers asked Eatherly if he would sign a secrecy agreement. He declined. He was a state employee on state duty, and although he would try to keep the secret as best he could, he simply couldn't do that, he told them.

Soon, they climbed out of the sinkhole and everyone got in their cars—Eatherly was not blindfolded on the way back—and the group retired to his motel room. There, they spent the next few hours looking at hundreds of Dean Kartchner's slide photos, stacked one on top of the other on Eatherly's bed. Eatherly was impressed. He had been to Carlsbad Caverns in New Mexico and to Blanchard Springs, Arkansas, just after the caverns in the Ozark National Forest had opened to the public in 1973, and he had some knowledge of the subject. "I could see right away just by looking at the decorations and the color on the slides that it was superb," he said.

After the Kartchners left, Tufts and Tenen asked Eatherly some questions. What would happen to them if State Parks agreed to take on the project? Would the two discoverers be able to influence the course of events? Eatherly essentially said no. The state would purchase it, and Xanadu would be in the State Parks agency's hands. Back in their own room, Tufts and Tenen sat on the floor on opposite sides, staring at each other. They had to make a decision. After some discussion, they decided that they had to go through with it. But they were still determined not to abdicate their role in the cave. "It was the best thing for the cave and really the only course we could take despite the risks," said Tufts. "It carried the possibility of permanent protection."

The following day, Eatherly returned to Phoenix, and Ed McCullough, who had suggested that Tufts contact State Parks, arrived to see the cave for himself. He had no trouble getting in and was enthralled. In a letter to then–Arizona State Parks executive director Michael Ramnes, dated February 5, McCullough touted the cave in the highest possible terms. "It is the most beautiful cave I have seen," he wrote. "It far surpasses the commercial caves now available to the public." It would be "a windfall opportunity for the state," he maintained. And he suggested that if Governor Babbitt would see the cave himself, "it would become a high priority on his list of state parks."

By this point, Tufts's trip around the world was on hold. In February, after Eatherly's visit and McCullough's letter, the two cavers went up to in Phoenix for a presentation to a group of the executive staff of Arizona State Parks including Eatherly, Executive Director Mike Ramnes, the deputy director, and various section heads. Tufts and Tenen showed slides of Xanadu and passed around some dusty cave mineral samples that they had purchased at rock shops; the idea was to show the pervasiveness of cave vandalism. They still hadn't let on exactly where the cave was, although two of the staffers quickly figured out its approximate location. There was a great deal of excitement at the meeting about what the agency was now referring to as "Secret Cave."

Yet Tufts and Tenen were not completely convinced. State Parks officials were expressing their reservations about whether secrecy could be maintained, even as they looked at samples of the kind of vandalism that could occur at Xanadu. And in follow-up phone conversations, Eatherly told Tenen, "We'll put it on the list," and seemed to dismiss Tufts with a polite "Thanks, Randy, we'll take it from here." The two discoverers grew even more alarmed, more so than that evening at the San Pedro Motel. "The implication was that State Parks would handle everything from that point on and that we needn't worry nor needn't be involved," said Tufts. "It was a bit like being asked to give up your

Cave bacon in the
Throne Room overlook
(K. L. Day, Arizona
State Parks)

child when they are only seven years old . . . If we were not involved—as gadflies at least—pushing wherever we could, things simply would not happen. The state bureaucracy, despite the best of intentions, simply could not move on this and do it quickly enough and in secret."

There was a feeling on their part that things were slipping out of their hands into those of bureaucrats who, despite their enthusiasm, didn't sufficiently appreciate the vulnerabilities of Xanadu and what could happen to the cave if word got out. Eatherly's implication that "Secret Cave" could wind up languishing on some list of potential park prospects didn't inspire much confidence either.

So Tufts and Tenen decided it was time to try another tack. They resolved to go straight to the top—to Governor Babbitt himself.

Going to the top, or to the source, was something that was a Randy Tufts characteristic. When Tufts read a book by an author he liked, he would call him up on the phone. That had been the case with Arthur M. Young, a mathematician and philosopher and author of books entitled *The Geometry of Meaning* and *The Reflexive Universe,* which tried to reconcile quantum physics and mysticism. Tufts was fascinated by the books, so he telephoned Young and drove to California to call on him. Back in 1977, during his hitchhiking trip in the East, Tufts had button-holed one of his heroes, the astronomer Carl Sagan. Unable to get an appointment to see the great man, he waited for four hours in a parking lot outside Sagan's office until Sagan emerged. "How might someone with a background in geology and community organizing find happiness in the space program?" he asked Sagan. The astronomer's reply: "I haven't the foggiest." The two agreed to correspond.

Similarly, when he had been student body president at the UA, Tufts had found himself dealing with the university president, with trustees, with state legislators. His refusal to be intimidated by famous and successful people was something that he had learned from his father Pete, who was in the public relations business and managed a number of political campaigns. Pete Tufts was at home with politicians and public officials and well-known people of all stripes, and so was his son.

So, with the assistance of Betsy Bolding, Babbitt's southern Arizona coordinator, he, Tenen, and Mark Kartchner found themselves in Governor Babbitt's office a month later. Babbitt had no idea why the trio had come to see him: his appointment book had simply blocked off time for some "Tucson community people," at Bolding's suggestion. To his visitors' amazement, on the wall of the governor's office was a painting of the Whetstone Mountains, done by Southwest artist Maynard Dixon. During the course of the conversation, Babbitt told them that the Whetstones were his favorite mountain range in the state. Although the painting didn't show the actual location of the cave, it came close—showing a view of the Whetstones viewed from the south from the Mustang Mountains. Tufts and Tenen took it as a sign.

Babbitt, forty-six at the time, was the kind of public official who was likely to be sympathetic. He had been a geology major in college and was a staunch environmentalist. (The Babbitts were an old northern Arizona ranching family who operated Indian trading posts in the 1880s and became prosperous Flagstaff merchants.) He was highly respected for his intellect. "He was always the smartest person in the room," said Dan Campbell, executive director of the Arizona Nature Conservancy at the time. And the governor was determined do something to upgrade the state parks system; the cave would be "a great way" to bring attention to the system, in Babbitt's view. Still, Babbitt wasn't about to commit himself to supporting the idea of making Xanadu a state park—yet. "I'll have to see it first," he said.

A few days later Babbitt spent a weekend in Sedona, where, amidst the red rock canyons, he huddled with his aides to determine his political future. At that meeting, Babbitt decided not to seek reelection as governor the following year but run for the 1988 Democratic nomination for president instead. He may have had more important things on his mind, to be sure, but he arrived at the meeting carrying with him a book on caves.

A date was set for Babbitt to visit Xanadu, but first Tufts and Tenen characteristically went through their list of "what ifs." Babbitt was unquestionably the most distinguished visitor the cave had ever had. They had no doubt but that the governor would be able to get into the cave successfully. The question was, if he injured himself inside, how would he get out? Or suppose someone else in his party needed to be rescued? "We had visions of having to drill holes in the top of the hill, of the National Guard coming in, of the media showing up, of thousands of people arriving at the cave," said Tenen. At the very minimum, there had to be a way to create a sufficiently wide passage to get a Stokes rescue litter into and out of the cave.

Tufts remembered that there was a small hole—about three inches in diameter—that extended from one of the rooms just off the sinkhole entrance into the area on the other side of the blowhole. The creation of a route through that hole could enable the governor to bypass the narrow blowhole crawlway. With the help of Bob Buecher, the experienced Tucson caver who had been brought on board, Tufts and Tenen rented a jackhammer and several hundred feet of compressor hose. Since compressor hose usually comes in twenty- to thirty-feet lengths—and no one store had the quantity they needed—they found themselves on a comic odyssey, wandering from store to store, gobbling up all the rentable compressor hose in Tucson. They spent an entire day jackhammering the hole open, snaking the hose through the wash up the hill into the cave. In the end, they constructed an alternative crawlway that would enable Babbitt and his party to enter and leave somewhat more easily, known subsequently as the "Babbitt Hole."

On April 14, the governor flew to Sierra Vista, the nearest airport to Xanadu. The arrival had all the trappings of a state visit. Babbitt brought with him with his two young sons, Christopher and T. J.; Betsy Bolding, his southern Arizona coordinator; Bernard Shanks, his chief adviser on environmental matters, and Shanks's son; and two Department of Public Safety officers. (Later that day, when Tenen was helping Babbitt's bodyguard Lori Norris down a slope inside the cave, he observed a re-volver strapped to her ankle.) Bob Buecher, experienced in cave rescue, and several Kartchners—who were physicians after all—were on hand in case anything went wrong. Bob Buecher's wife Debbie, an experi-enced caver in her own right, and Ed McCullough, the UA dean who had encouraged Tufts to approach State Parks, were also present. The day was completely blank on the governor's calendar. For a number of hours—four of them spent inside the cave—no one had any idea where he was.

The governor and his party entered without incident, "scrambling down the hole, belly-flopping into the cave," as Babbitt put it. The Bab-bitt Hole was a success. Babbitt toured the front of the cave, includ-ing the Big Room, but the party didn't make it all the way back to the Throne Room, with Kubla Khan and the cave's most dramatic sites; that would have been too arduous. "It was really incredible," said Babbitt. "I've been in my share of caves. But this was a wet cave. You felt that you were there in the process of creation. It was in motion, still forming."

Yet when Babbitt emerged from the cave into the light of day, he was visibly tired, even as the discoverers continued peppering him with information and descriptions of Xanadu's wonders. And he was still making no promises.

A few days later, Tufts and Tenen received a note from the governor, thanking them for providing "a priceless adventure" and "a splendid outing." Babbitt continued, "I now better understand and admire the deep concern and dedication you have for the valuable resource which has become your 'career project.'" The letter was signed "Bruce" but made no commitments.

Still, the Babbitt trip had some immediate positive effects. In the wake of the governor's visit, Tufts and Tenen were put in touch with two people associated with The Nature Conservancy, the environmental organization that had a track record of acquiring parkland and wildlife areas on behalf of various government agencies. (During the sometimes drawn-out time frame when the government tries to appropriate funds

to buy land, the price can skyrocket; with this in mind, the Conservancy purchases and holds the land for government agencies until the acquisition goes through, keeping the price down and protecting the property at the same time.) Bill Roe was a Tucson philanthropist who had been chairman of the Arizona Nature Conservancy's board; Babbitt had famously called him the "environmental hair shirt of the state of Arizona." Dan Campbell was the Arizona Nature Conservancy's new executive director. The idea was that either the Conservancy might purchase the cave outright or do so on behalf of Arizona State Parks or, if that didn't work out, on behalf of some other entity.

At first, Roe was wary of Tufts and Tenen. They met at a corner of the bar at the posh Arizona Inn in the university area of Tucson. "They kept looking over their shoulders to make sure no one was looking," Roe recalled. Tufts and Tenen showed him one photo of the cave after another. At one point Roe told him he had seen enough. But they insisted, "We can't move on to the next stage until you've seen all the pictures!"

Shortly afterwards, Roe went to Xanadu with his wife and two children. Like Eatherly's, the trip had a cloak-and-dagger quality to it. Tufts and Tenen called him the day before and told him where to leave his car; they would pick him up at that spot and take him to the cave. Roe

Formations just off the end of the Big Room (Steve Holland)

left a sealed envelope with a friend. If the friend hadn't heard from Roe by midnight, he was supposed to open the envelope which would reveal the location of Roe's car. Tufts and Tenen were "so paranoid and protective," Roe recalled. "There was an element of 'Are these guys completely sane or not?'" By signing the secrecy agreement, Roe managed to avoid having to wear a blindfold, however.

At least some of Roe's misgivings were justified. On the way into the cave, he got stuck in the blowhole crawlway for what seemed like an eternity, and "saw [his] life flash before [his] eyes"; finally, with Tufts and Tenen entreating him to relax and elongate his body, he was able to free himself. Still, he found his visit "a remarkable adventure." And he was impressed enough to arrange financing for Tufts, Tenen, and an official from State Parks to go to a cave management conference in Blanchard Springs, Arkansas. In those days, agencies like State Parks were prohibited from spending their own monies to finance travel by their employees out-of-state, a policy that baffled Tufts and Tenen, intensifying their doubts about state participation. "We wanted to set the highest standard for the cave and State Parks officials couldn't even leave the state!" noted Tenen.

Arizona Nature Conservancy Executive Director Campbell had misgivings of a different sort. He was skeptical of the idea that the way to save the cave was to open it to the public. That was certainly not in line with the Conservancy's principles and traditional approach. "When we buy things, we buy things expressly to protect them," he said. "Oftentimes to do that, we don't encourage a lot of visitation." It took a while to convince him that unless you guarded the cave twenty-four hours a day, you couldn't protect it. "Why not just close it up?" he asked Tufts and Tenen at the initial meeting held at his Tucson office. "Bats live there," they replied. Why not put a gate instead? "People with dynamite and hammers will go right through." Campbell was eventually convinced.

Another problem, though, involved The Nature Conservancy's own strict policies toward acquisitions. Any land that it purchased had to involve a biological imperative—some kind of endangered species or rare biological habitat. Otherwise, the Conservancy had no mandate to get involved. The vulnerable *Myotis velifer* bats that roosted at Xanadu every spring and summer provided the necessary justification. "The bats, they were the cue," said Campbell.

Clearly, the next step was to talk to the Kartchners to get an idea of the price they might accept for the cave. Roe was assigned to the task. The Kartchners told him they wanted $1.5 million for the land and $1.5 million for the cave. Almost immediately, they thought better of it: they wanted $3 million for the cave. As Campbell put it somewhat wryly, "After hearing from Gary and Randy for years that their cave was

Bill Roe, philanthropist and chairman of Arizona's Nature Conservancy Board. He found his cave trip "a remarkable adventure." (Gary Tenen)

'priceless,' when it came time to actually negotiate the purchase, it was no surprise that their estimate of the cave's value was 'priceless.'"

The Nature Conservancy had an ace in the hole in negotiating with the Kartchners: Governor Babbitt. Campbell was able to assure them that, once a price had been decided, if there was a snag and the state wouldn't come up with all the money, the governor would guarantee whatever sum was finally agreed to. "I didn't have the money personally," said Babbitt. "But it was typical of me to say, 'If the state doesn't move, I'll raise the money.' We would have started a campaign. We did a fair amount of that. It would be quite easy to raise money." The governor did admit, however, that it might be trickier here than in other situations because the amount of money required involved not just buying the property, but also developing the cave itself.

Still, no one had any idea what the cave was worth. So Roe and Campbell looked around to recruit a knowledgeable person to evaluate it. Finding someone who did appraisals on what Campbell called "a black hole in the ground" wasn't easy; it obviously was not a service that was called for everyday. They found their man in H. C. "Bud" Cannon of St. George, Utah. Cannon had done appraisals of islands, mountaintops, and hot springs. When Tufts first telephoned and asked how he would appraise a cave, Cannon told him that the value would be found by calculating the volume of the interior of the cave, multiplied by the tons of bat guano therein, divided by the number of miles from the nearest city of a population over 130,420, multiplied by the element of secrecy involved, all measured on a scale of one to ten. Tufts was not amused.

The fact was that Cannon had never appraised a cave. But he soon set to work, using other show caves like the Caverns of Sonora in West Texas as his "comparables." As Campbell noted, there were lots of questions that came into play. Did the Kartchners own all the land above the cavern? (The answer was yes.) Did The Nature Conservancy need to negotiate with the next-door federal landowners? (No.) Could cave features be considered mineral rights—if so, under federal law, the caves belonged to the U.S. government. (The answer was that cave features are not considered "metalliferous minerals," so this was not an issue.) The Nature Conservancy footed the bill for the appraisal.

While Cannon was casting about for comparables, Tucson cavers Bob and Debbie Buecher embarked on an assessment of Xanadu in relation to other caves around the state and the country. It was a subjective assessment, but the Buechers had been to 150 caves in Arizona and had gone on over five hundred trips to caves; they had also done studies for Mammoth Cave and Carlsbad Caverns. Clearly, they knew what they were talking about. Using a one-to-ten rating system and comparing everything from the location of particular caves to various formations such as helictites, cave popcorn, and gypsum flowers, the Buechers matched up Xanadu against various commercial and "wild," undeveloped caves. Although Xanadu was ranked not as impressive in overall features as Carlsbad Caverns in New Mexico and the Caverns of Sonora, its location was better; anyway, its features surpassed any other Arizona commercial caves. (Its features also surpassed those of Mammoth Cave in Kentucky, known for its vast size but not for its cave decorations.) Overall, the Buechers' rating made the state and The Nature Conservancy happy; Xanadu was a valuable resource that could

Soda straws and helictites in the Throne Room overlook (K. L. Day, Arizona State Parks)

stand on its own versus other caves. Whether it justified the price that the Kartchners were asking was another matter.

After the years of limbo and the first, cautious approach to State Parks and the Eatherly visit, things were happening quickly. But time was still not on Tufts and Tenen's side. In July 1985, a few months after Babbitt's trip to the cave, Gary Tenen was sitting in his office at AlphaGraphics when there was a knock on the door. His visitor was a prominent member of the Tucson grotto named Steve Holland. "I want to tell you about a cave," Holland said. Tenen scrunched up his face. "What cave?" he asked.

Holland had been involved in caving in Tucson ever since junior high school. And, like most cavers in the secretive Escabrosa Grotto, he was always "listening for intelligence," in his words. Years before, in 1980, he had been on a caving trip with four other people in New Mexico. Holland was standing at the top of a pit, ready to rappel, when he heard the two cavers who had already descended talking about a cave they called "CJ" and how someone—he couldn't make out who—had "gotten in trouble for taking someone to CJ." When Holland arrived at the bottom of the pit and de-rigged his descending gear, he asked them, jokingly, "When are we going to CJ?" There was a long pause, and one of the cavers replied, "Don't go asking about CJ!" That caver was Scott Davis, one of the earlier group who had gotten into Xanadu and received a late-night warning from Gary Tenen. "CJ"—or Cracker-jack—the early name for Xanadu, had gotten its name from a Cracker Jack box found at the entrance.

After that snippet of overheard information, the dogged Holland spent hours at the University of Arizona library, pouring through topographical maps, looking for anything with the initials "CJ" on it. He found no clues. But over the years he had heard rumors about a "world-record soda straw formation" and a "cave on private land." He had also heard a rumor that Gary Tenen had found an incredible cave somewhere and had blown the entrance shut with dynamite. Holland never gave the latter rumor much credence, however. It was just "caving folklore bullcrap," he was sure.

Flash forward to 1985. Holland had a friend who was a geology student and who proposed a ridge-walking expedition in the limestone foothills on the east side of the Whetstones. The two went out there one day and found themselves within a few hundred yards of the entrance of the Xanadu sinkhole, although they weren't aware of it at the time. A few days later Holland was on the phone with Scott Davis—who had

Caver Steve Holland peers through the blowhole on a later visit (K. L. Day, Arizona State Parks)

warned him off "CJ" five years before—telling him about their latest trip. "Maybe that is where Gary Tenen blew up his secret cave!" Holland said jokingly. The usually garrulous Davis was strangely quiet on the other end of the phone, and then a light bulb went off in Holland's head. He asked Davis if the area where they had been hiking might have anything to do with another secret cave he had heard about some years earlier, namely "CJ." "You'd better go talk to Gary," Davis told him.

Holland was so intrigued that the very next morning he drove out to the Whetstones by himself, parked on the highway, hopped the fence, and walked right up to what turned out be the actual entrance of the cave. He let himself down the sinkhole and went into the initial rooms far enough to see a blockade of rocks. He realized he hadn't just come close to "CJ"—he had found it.

The next day, he made an appointment with Tenen. He wanted to return a radiator hose that he owed him from an earlier trip, he told him. That day in Tenen's office, Holland described the location and the entrance of the cave exactly. Tenen hesitated. Clearly, here was someone who knew enough to be a real danger to the secret of the cave. If Tenen denied the whole thing, he would lose some degree of control. On the other hand, if he told Holland the truth, he could bring him in, make him a kind of "partner." Tenen knew Holland to be a trustworthy person. He pulled out a map of Xanadu and unrolled it. "Oh, you mean *this* cave!" he said with a huge grin on his face. A few nights later, Tufts came by Holland's house. He had him sign a secrecy agreement and reiterated the entire story—the governor's visit, the possible deal involving The Nature Conservancy and Arizona State Parks, the sensitivity of the situation. Holland had been taken into the "circle of confidence."

A few weeks later, Holland learned that a group of his friends had been digging in some small cave entrances in the Whetstones. In the mesquite-covered wash not far from the sinkhole, they had found what appeared to be a second, collapsed entrance to Xanadu. They were planning another expedition to dig there, without realizing there already was an entrance. Would Holland like to go along?

Holland was faced with a dilemma. He didn't want to betray his friends, but on the other hand, he knew that if word got out about Xanadu, the consequences could be disastrous, undermining the original discoverers' years of planning. He paid another visit to Tenen. Tufts and Tenen asked if he would be willing to pretend to go along with the idea and funnel back any information to them; he would essentially function as a "mole" in the operation. In the meantime, Tenen, Tufts, and the Kartchners would concoct a plan to scare the interlopers away. Holland reluctantly agreed.

When the day came for their caving trip, Holland informed Tenen what time the group would arrive at the cave. The five cavers, including Holland, showed up at the second entrance and began to dig. They spent two hours with picks and shovels, extending the passage eight to ten feet. As this was going on, Holland was getting increasingly impatient—there was no sign of Tufts, Tenen, or the Kartchners. He already felt caught in the middle, and now the plan didn't seem to be working out. Two cavers were standing outside, while the others were digging inside, when they heard the sound of horses' hoofs. As if out of a John Ford Western, three Kartchner brothers suddenly appeared on horseback, one of them with a pistol hanging from his belt. "Didn't you notice the sign?" one of the brothers demanded, in a none-too-friendly tone, referring to the "No trespassing" markers that the family had placed every six hundred feet around the property. "Yes," said one of the cavers meekly. The reply: "Then go back and read it again!" The brothers took down everyone's name, including Holland's, and the cavers departed.

"They certainly didn't look like doctors," said Holland of the Kartchner brothers. "They looked like ranch folk."

During the journey back to Tucson, the interlopers were clearly annoyed by what had happened. Holland, sitting quietly and perhaps feeling a little guilty, gave no hint of his role in the whole affair. At that point, his fellow cavers had no idea that he was a "secret agent"; they assumed that the arrival of the Kartchner brothers was purely coincidental, that the owners of the property were just out for a weekend gallop around their land. If they had known that one of their own had betrayed them, they would have been furious. "It was the lesser of two evils," Holland said. "If there was a leak, it could compromise the deal [between the state and the Kartchner family]." On that ride home, the group decided, just like Scott Davis and his friends five years before, that it simply wasn't worth pursuing any further explorations on Kartchner property.

———————————

By the fall of 1985, Tufts was finally ready to leave on the long-delayed trip around the world. It seemed the opportune time to go: the state was interested and involved in "Secret Cave," the appraiser was methodically going about his work, The Nature Conservancy was on board. He still wasn't sure in what direction to take his life, how much he wanted to devote himself to Xanadu. He needed to think about these things—and what better place to do this than half a world away from Tucson?

Before leaving, in a letter dated November 20, 1985, he left his sister Judy his last instructions, in case of his death—that "once in a lifetime experience, not to be missed." First he wanted a party, with lots of Guinness beer. Then, if there were any remains, "have them cremated and scattered on Xanadu hill over the Throne Room and the Big Room." Hopefully, his surviving molecules would "percolate down and become part of the cave formations." The scatterers of his ashes should be limited to a small trusted group—he was still worrying about keeping the whereabouts of the cave secret—including Tenen, of course. He wanted a simple service, perhaps with Dean Kartchner, a Mormon bishop, as the leader. "Well, I always wanted to be able to find all the caves in the Whetstones and this would allow me to do that," he wrote. "My ghost will attempt to preserve appropriately any caves so found. Ahem. . . . It should be fun. So be of good cheer."

Soon after, he left for his first stop: Hawaii.

The Stars Line Up

RANDY TUFTS WAS GONE for fourteen months. In Hawaii, he viewed the eruption of Kilauea, the world's most active volcano, camping out alone in a rain forest just a mile from where it was spewing molten lava. In the Philippines, it was politics, not geology, that captured his attention, as he watched Corazon Aquino lead her fellow countrymen in street protests against the regime of dictator Ferdinand Marcos. In Hong Kong, when he determined that his camera wasn't taking sufficiently sharp pictures, Tufts wandered into a bookstore, found a book of photos he liked, and immediately telephoned the author (who fortuitously lived in Hong Kong) to find out what kind of camera he had used; Tufts then went out and bought the identical one. In Pakistan's remote North West Frontier Province, he matched shooting skills with local tribesmen. He visited India, Egypt, and Israel.

In a letter to friends in Denver from Hong Kong, dated July 12, 1986, Tufts wrote, "Traveling my way has so far been highly introspective. A 'what am I am doing with my life' quest. For so long I've felt a bit lost, having left geology for a murky, undefined political realm where little was connected and everything was intangible. That's why I quit my job . . . [At this point] I'm seeing many things more clearly, and accepting things about which there may never be any clarity. I'm seeing fascinating places—where travel agents fear to tread—and meeting nice and memorable people. All and all—just what I needed."

In Pakistan, in the summer of 1986, he received word from Gary Tenen telling him that James A. Kartchner, the patriarch of the Kartchner clan, had died of Alzheimer's disease. As he continued on his travels, there were other disturbing developments at home. Bruce Babbitt was no longer Arizona's governor, having left office to run for the president of the United States instead; his replacement, self-made businessman Evan Mecham, was considered no friend of the environment. The Arizona State Parks agency was in disarray, with a changing cast of characters in leadership positions. The agency director had left, to be replaced with another, who would soon leave himself. With lack of support from the top, Bud Cannon slowed his appraisal process, frustrating the Kartchners. Demoralization set in, particularly on the Kartchner side: James A. Kartchner, the great proponent of the cave, was dead; the appraisal process was stymied and the state role in question; Tufts was exploring the world; Tenen was absorbed in his business and family. And, in the Kartchner family's judgment, too many people appeared to know about the cave anyway—there was just no guarantee of its security.

So the Kartchners decided to take a radical step: they would seal the entrance of Xanadu for twenty years. In early 1987, family members took their last expeditions to the cave, video trips intended to be a sort of swan song. Meanwhile, they measured the dimensions of the sinkhole and drew up designs for a cover made of iron rails and corrugated plating. "We were feeling frustration and futility," said Mark Kartchner. "All we needed was a hand mixer and gravel and cement [to make the seal]. We were prepared to rent a Bobcat loader." Mark was sure that he could get a license to use explosives.

By the spring and summer of 1987, the Kartchner family was a month or so away from carrying out its plan.

But, just as the situation looked hopeless, the winds began to shift again. In April of that year, Kenneth E. Travous became the executive director of Arizona State Parks. He was the third director in three years. Travous had been deputy director of the agency for a year, a job that was largely administrative; he had never heard of a cave in the Whetstone Mountains that might make a good state park. But for some of his deputies—Charles Eatherly among them—"Secret Cave" remained a top priority. "There are two guys in Tucson who you have got to talk to but we can't tell you what about," they told him. Travous was intrigued.

A month after Travous's ascension to the State Parks directorship, Randy Tufts returned home from his trip. He had decided to come back to Tucson and intensify his involvement with the cave. He moved in with the Tenens, staying in their guest bedroom, where he covered the bed with piles of newspapers and photos—transforming it into an "auxiliary desk"—and insisted on sleeping on the floor in the same sleeping bag he had used in his travels around the world. Tufts met with the Kartchner brothers to tell them of his new commitment. However, he found them disillusioned and still determined to go through with their plan to seal Xanadu.

It was only in July of that year that Tufts and Tenen even learned that Ken Travous existed. They had tried to get in touch with the previous State Parks executive director, only to be told that someone new had taken his place. A few weeks later the pair met Travous at a quiet table in the back of the Woods Memorial Branch Library on First Avenue in

Arizona State Parks Executive Director Ken Travous (right) with Gary Tenen and Randy Tufts (Gary Tenen)

Tucson. "They didn't know me from Adam," Travous recalled. "I don't know that they had much hope that anyone in Phoenix was going to help them, and I don't say as I blame them." But Travous, like Bruce Babbitt before him, was determined to breathe new life into the State Parks agency. "Secret Cave" might turn out to be the key.

Soon enough, he was crawling on his belly through the Babbitt Hole, the first time an Arizona State Parks director had ventured into the cave. And he was impressed by what he saw. "Inside, it was hot and humid and it was work," Travous said. "When we stood up and started popping into different areas and you could see things, then I started getting excited. I got a sense for the size of it. But you still didn't understand. It kept getting bigger and bigger and more beautiful."

The story also goes that on his first visit to Xanadu, Travous was resting his arms on a scraggly mesquite tree just outside the sinkhole, chatting with Tufts, Tenen, and the Kartchners. Despite his usually relaxed demeanor, Travous was a little apprehensive that day; it was a critical first meeting, after all, with both the Kartchners and the cave. Then he heard the voice of one of the Kartchner brothers telling him with unexpected firmness, "Walk toward me! Slowly!" He did as he was told and then turned around to see a black-tailed rattler sitting in the tree he had just been leaning against. The party went into the cave, and when they came out, everyone asked him, "What did you think of it?" Travous replied, "You've got one problem." The group held its collective breath. "Something darn mean is scaring rattlesnakes into that tree!"

Travous very quickly grasped the vulnerability of the cave's geographic situation, in a way that other people at the agency hadn't. "My first thoughts were that this is real close to a highway and if they didn't do something, it could be found again," he said. "This isn't one hundred miles in the middle of nowhere."

The new executive director also shared the strong conservation and stewardship ethic that Tufts and Tenen espoused. When he was growing up in southern Illinois, his grandfather would take him on hunting trips. Soon he started to go on his own, walking through the deep woods at ages nine and ten. One muggy August morning he sat down under a large walnut tree. He remembered it this way: "The tree was big and beautiful and I thought, 'No one has ever sat here before' and then I looked and there was a tin can. And that just ruined it. Someone had been there and they didn't care!" At that moment, he says, he started wondering, "Are there places left, where you are the first one? And what do you need to do to keep them that way?"

At "Secret Cave," he was convinced that he had found what he had been looking for. "Thirty years later I found myself in this place where Randy and Gary didn't throw a beer can," he said. "They treated it with utmost respect. That gave me my reward."

Travous was on board. And he brought considerable political skills to the task. He was persuasive and good-humored, with a folksy charm, possessing just the right touch with legislators and the bureaucracy. And he was absolutely determined to make "Secret Cave" happen. Although he only had a glimmer of this at the time, it was going to be the making of his agency—and of his own career.

One of the first things Travous did was to talk to the Kartchners. He apologized for the neglect, the poor communication, the general inertia that had characterized the State Parks agency for the previous year and a half. With a new director at the helm, this was all going to change, he assured them. Family members decided to give him a chance; they put the idea of sealing the cave to one side and returned to the appraisal process.

Then, Travous paid a call on Joe Lane, the Speaker of the Arizona House of Representatives, at Lane's office at the Capitol. If the state were

Angel's Wing shield
(K. L. Day, Arizona
State Parks)

to acquire the cave as a state park, Lane's support would be essential. Lane was a Republican, like all the legislative leaders during this period. Previously parliamentarian and majority whip, he had been in the leadership for a number of years and was known for his plainspoken and forthright manner. A cattleman and former president of the Arizona Cattle Growers Association, Lane hailed from Willcox, a Cochise County town northeast of Benson that advertised itself as the home of the singing cowboy movie actor Rex Allen. By sheer coincidence, "Secret Cave" was in his district. "That is what got my attention," Lane said.

Travous brought along his deputy, Courtland Nelson, and twelve photos of Xanadu, "all covered up and mysterious," as Lane recalled. The State Parks executive director shut the door. "Let me show you something," he said. With every picture, Lane's eyes got wider and wider. The Speaker himself had been to Carlsbad Caverns in New Mexico as a youngster and to Mammoth Cave in Kentucky during World War II. He considered himself a "cave nut." He was stunned that a natural wonder of this caliber was lying under a hillside somewhere in a part of the state he knew so well; the economic benefits for his district could be immense. "We didn't have any major tourist destinations in southern Arizona," Lane noted. "We had no Grand Canyon or anything like that. As soon as I saw the pictures, I began to see this wasn't like Colossal Cave in Tucson. This was a big deal. Dollar signs just went around in my head. It would be a big tourism boon for southern Arizona."

One of the first things that Lane wanted to know was how much the cave would cost to develop. Travous conceded that he didn't know but was sure the cave would be such an attraction that it would pay for itself. Lane was carried away by his own enthusiasm for the photos and dreams of "dollar signs." He told the State Parks executive director he could count on him.

And so Travous took a handful of legislators into his confidence, legislators who would be key if the idea had a chance of going anywhere. Secrecy was still the overriding concern that somehow had to be maintained throughout the lengthy legislative process; everyone seemed to understand that. The emotional burden of secrecy, transferred from Tufts and Tenen to the Kartchners and then to State Parks, was now being passed on to the leaders of the legislature. Next on Travous's list was Carl Kunasek, the retired Mesa pharmacist who was Senate president.

Shields and soda straws in the Mushroom Passage (K. L. Day, Arizona State Parks)

State Representative
Larry Hawke (left)
and Arizona Nature
Conservancy Executive
Director Dan Campbell
at the cave site
(Gary Tenen)

Then, Travous told John Hays, the head of the Senate Natural Resources
and Agriculture Committee, as well as his opposite number in the
House, Larry Hawke, a Tucson Republican, who was chair of the House
Natural Resources and Energy Committee. Hays was one of the largest
cattle ranchers in northern Arizona, and Hawke was a third-generation
Tucsonan; by another stroke of luck, both men were on the board of
trustees of The Nature Conservancy, which was intimately involved in
the matter. Any legislation would originate in their committees.

Shortly thereafter, Lane and Hawke joined Travous, Tufts, and Tenen
at a secret meeting in Patagonia, south of Tucson, as part of a legislative
tour of southern Arizona parks, sponsored by The Nature Conservancy.
There, Tufts and Tenen met the legislators for the first time. Members of
the Arizona State Parks Board and a Cochise County supervisor were
among those present, as was Representative Hawke's nine-year-old son
Tommy. Hawke remembers that some people signed secrecy agreements
at the meeting; he didn't—as a legislator he thought he was "exempt."
Hawke's young son asked, "Do I have to sign?" "No," his father told him.
"But it is important that you not say anything until the time is appropri-

ate." Tommy Hawke, a Cub Scout, Eagle Scout, and later a Tucson police officer, never told a soul until news of the cave went public.

At that meeting Hawke told Tufts, "This couldn't have been in a better place if the Chamber of Commerce had decided where the cave was going to be."

One person who was not told about the cave, however, was Governor Evan Mecham. For 1987 and 1988 were very bitter and divisive years in the politics of the state of Arizona, culminating in the impeachment of the governor. Mecham, the owner of a Pontiac car dealership in the Phoenix suburb of Glendale, had run four previous times for the state's top office before being elected in 1986. An ultra-conservative Republican and former Mormon lay bishop, Mecham created instant controversy by canceling Martin Luther King Jr.'s birthday as a paid holiday for state workers. In one of his famously insensitive quotes, he said, "I'm not a racist. . . . I employ them [blacks] because they are the best people who applied for the cotton picking job"; he also defended his use of the word, "pickaninny." Cancellation of the King holiday was a decision that wreaked havoc on the state's tourism industry, resulting in a nationwide boycott in which some two hundred organizations moved conventions and meetings out of Arizona, depriving the state of millions of dollars in revenues. The governor's behavior became increasingly erratic, even paranoid, and his relationship with many of his fellow Republicans in the legislature went from bad to worse.

In January 1988, just three days before the governor's annual State of the State address, Mecham was indicted on six felony counts that included concealing a political contribution of $350,000 received from a lawyer under investigation by the attorney general in an alleged arbitrage scam. He was also accused of borrowing $80,000 from the governor's Protocol Fund to bail out his financially troubled auto dealership; this was not part of the legal indictment, however. Even before the indictment, an effort to recall him from office was underway in shopping malls and movie theaters across the state, garnering 391,738 signatures, 175,000 more than required. At the beginning of 1988, impeachment proceedings began in the legislature. The Republican Party was badly fractured on the issue, with Barry Goldwater, dean of Arizona Republicans, calling for Mecham's ouster. But Mecham had his loyal supporters—particularly among many of the state's fellow Mormons—who believed the governor's accusations that the downtown Phoenix business establishment was out to destroy him. With the six-count indictment, recall campaign, and impeachment proceedings, "Every lawful means to oust Evan Mecham was in place by the anniversary of his inauguration," wrote Ronald J. Watkins in his book *High Crimes and*

Misdemeanors. "The only steps not taken were armed insurrection and assassination."

It was in this heated, even poisonous, political atmosphere that Ken Travous first approached Joe Lane about finding a way to get the state legislature to purchase "Secret Cave" and turn it into an Arizona state park. As Speaker of the House, Lane was deeply enmeshed in the impeachment process; constitutionally, it was the Speaker's job to initiate impeachment proceedings. According to Watkins's book, impeachment had made Lane "the recipient of more abuse than any public official in state history." Given everything that was going on, it wasn't totally surprising when Lane remarked to Travous at that first meeting, "This is the best news I've had in months!"

But the Speaker was under no illusions that the acquisition of "Secret Cave" would be easy, especially in the midst of the passions and divisions of impeachment. "In the legislature, nothing is secret," said Lane. "You are starting with an impossible task. If we were talking about a hundred thousand bucks, it would be no big deal. We could have slipped it through with nobody asking questions. But we were talking about millions of dollars. And it was right in the middle of a time when nobody trusted anybody—the time of impeachment! We had a certain percentage of the legislature—maybe 10 or 15 percent, maybe higher than that—who didn't trust the leadership at all."

How then to get a bill through the legislature totally distracted by impeaching the governor and how to do so without anyone knowing or at least without knowing the specifics or the cost?

"What we did—the three or four of us who knew—was sit down to work out a strategy," said Lane. "The key was trust. It had to be trust by everybody involved."

The strategy was a simple one. The cave proponents would introduce a seemingly innocuous bill having to do with State Parks funding—without any mention of the acquisition of "Secret Cave"—and start it moving through the legislative process. The legislation would establish an Acquisition and Development (A&D) fund that would enable Arizona State Parks to tap revenues from user fees and concessions to acquire and develop property for parkland; essentially the bill would let the State Parks agency keep some of its own money. The Speaker of the House and the Senate President and the leaders of the relevant committees—in this case, John Hays on the Senate side and Larry Hawke in the House—would know the true intent of the legislation, but almost no one else would. The Senate and the House would pass slightly different versions of the bill, however, so at the very end of the process, the legislation would have to go to a Senate-House conference committee. There it would be amended to include the acquisition of the cave, and the secret would finally be out just before it went back to the full Senate and House for a final vote.

"The strategy was that we wanted as few people to know as possible until the last possible moment," said Hawke. "And we wanted to build momentum among gatekeepers and policy makers."

In legislative parlance, the name for this kind of legislation is "a vehicle bill." Hawke explained it this way: "It has to be a bill that is moving but it can't have its own baggage. It is like a limousine with no one in it, so you can get from point A to point B. You want a bill that is not in itself [so] controversial that it will drag down the new issue," in this case, the acquisition of the cave. If the bill was amended in committee too early, its true intent would be exposed before the sponsors were ready; if amended on the floor before it was ready, it would have the same problem. Timing was crucial. The key was to keep it in its most innocuous and non-controversial form until the Senate-House conference committee met toward the very end of the process. In that way, secrecy could be preserved; the cave would be protected while the complex legislative process was going on. The question, as Hawke put it, was "How long can we carry the thing before we had to spill it?"

It was hardly the first time this legislative tactic had been used in Arizona or in any other state. But one thing was characteristic of this approach—the public had no knowledge of, or role in, it whatsoever.

At the same moment that the "vehicle bill" was wending its way through the legislature, the House was drafting articles of impeachment against Governor Mecham. Once that was completed, the Senate would sit as a court. The legislators and the public were in a near-uproar, their attention focused almost entirely on the fate of their governor. The "Secret Cave" strategy took this all into consideration. With the House busy drawing up articles of impeachment, the piece of legislation, Senate Bill 1188, would originate in John Hays's Senate committee. Once the full Senate approved it, it would be sent over to Larry Hawke's House committee. By then, the House would have finished its impeachment work, and the Senate would just be preparing the trial. Impeachment and Bill 1188 would cross the Senate-House boundary line at the same time, each heading in the opposite direction.

That was the strategy, but the outcome was never certain. There could be snags, unexpected developments, leaks, especially in the volatile impeachment atmosphere. "Weirdness can happen up there," said Hawke.

To avoid some of the potential for "weirdness," a decision had been made early in the process not to tell Governor Mecham. "We didn't trust him or his minions that hung around him," Speaker Lane said. "I got along fine with Mecham. He had no social graces at all, no easy way to say no, and had a personality that got him in trouble. The guys hanging around him were scum. So we didn't let any of them know what was going on. They'd have blown it for sure."

However, in his position as Arizona State Parks executive director, Ken Travous was required to have periodic contact with the governor and his staff. So when Travous and his deputies would meet with various people in Mecham's office, they would ask general questions like, "If Governor Mecham was interested in a new park in Arizona, what kind of park would he be interested in?" "Inane, stupid stuff," as Travous put it. The idea was just to let the governor know, in the vaguest terms, that something was afoot, just in case Mecham survived impeachment and they had to enlist his backing. One reason, Travous says, that he and his aides didn't want to tell anyone on Mecham's staff was that, in this time of turmoil, "we didn't know if they were going to be there the next day. I would go and have a meeting with a liaison in the governor's office at 5 p.m. and read in the papers the next day that that person had left. That kind of thing was going on all the time. It was just chaos."

Before the legislative process could go forward, there was one crucial matter to attend to, however. Arizona State Parks, with the help of The Nature Conservancy, had to reach an agreement with the Kartchners on the price of the cave and the surrounding property. Appraiser Bud Cannon had stepped up his work, visiting show caves around the country to establish "comparables," trying to pry financial information out of closed-mouthed cave owners. Now, he had decided on a final figure. So, in February 1988, in a windowless sleeping room deep in the bowels of St. Joseph's Hospital in Tucson, the Arizona Nature Conservancy's executive director, Dan Campbell, met with a group of Kartchner brothers. Four brothers came to the meeting, two of them still between shifts at the hospital and attired in surgical scrubs. Campbell sat at a desk; the brothers sat on the bed and a couple of borrowed chairs. The Nature Conservancy executive director was anxious. He knew that the Kartchners had unrealistic expectations, believing that their cave and the property surrounding it might be worth as much as $5 million, far more than the appraisal was likely to come in at.

Instead, the appraisal for the 160 acres containing the cave turned out to be much less—$1.3 million, Campbell told them. The surrounding 390 acres of grazing property were determined to be worth another $500,000, for a total appraised value of $1.8 million. Campbell asked the family if they would be willing to forego a portion of the total appraisal for a final price of $1.625 million. That was a "bargain sale," as it was known, offering the Kartchners some tax benefits, while at the same time saving the state some money. The plan was for the Conservancy to buy the property on behalf of the state of Arizona, once it gained legislative approval. To make the deal more palatable to the family, a pie-shaped piece of ranchland just across State Highway 90 from the cave was excluded from the sale; this potentially lucrative property would remain in the hands of the Kartchners. (Tufts and Tenen were involved in putting together that part of the agreement.) In another "sweetener," Campbell told the Kartchners that Arizona State Parks had decided to name its new property James and Lois Kartchner State Park.

After Campbell told them the news, the brothers huddled together for what seemed to Campbell an eternity and told him they would get back to him. Meanwhile, Campbell walked out into the late-morning sunshine, still nervous, and not very optimistic. "I knew they had a large family, lots of college tuitions, and lots of hopes for 'cashing out,'" he said.

A few days later, the Kartchners agreed to the appraiser's and Campbell's terms.

The Kartchner family, said Larry Hawke, was "a class act. Sharp, sharp, sharp. You couldn't have picked a better family to own that property."

Randy Tufts put it this way: "[T]he Kartchners were modest despite their significant achievements. The offspring had not asked for the name designation for themselves, although they appreciated the acknowledgment it would be to their parents.

"The Kartchners had started with a teacher's salary and a tithe of eight eggs [that Mrs. Kartchner's family had paid to the Mormon church at a particularly low point in the family's fortunes]. Now they were contemplating selling a section of their land for 1.5 million dollars. But, given the large number of ways the Kartchners would have to divide the proceeds, no one would get rich. In fact, considering what they valued in life, the funds would more likely help pay educational expenses for seventy grandchildren and nineteen great-grandchildren than it would buy fast cars and stereos . . .

"The family had shouldered the unexpected responsibility of stewardship. For the physicians assembled there with Campbell, and for all their relatives, the teachers, the home workers, the contributing members of a multitude of communities, it was all in a day's work."

As planned, in January 1988, Senator Hays introduced Senate Bill 1188, calling for the establishment of the State Parks agency's A&D fund but with no mention of "Secret Cave." It passed his Natural Resources and Agriculture Committee and moved on to the Senate Rules Committee, before a vote of the full Senate. On February 8, the Arizona House delivered three articles of impeachment of Governor Mecham to the Senate. Mecham's impeachment trial in the upper chamber would begin on February 29. It was essential that Bill 1188 get out of the Senate before that happened or it would be dead for the session. Then, Travous got a call from Senator Hays. It seemed that Senator Jack Taylor, chairman of the Appropriations Committee, "smelled a rat." Although an important committee chair, Taylor had not been informed of the true nature of the "vehicle" that was passing through his committee. To the canny Taylor, it made no sense that the leadership was pushing so hard for a mere A&D bill when something as momentous as impeachment was happening. Alarmed, Travous grabbed the same photos he had shown to Joe Lane a few months before, stuffed them in his briefcase, and hurried down to Taylor's office. "You're right, Senator," the State Parks executive director told him. "There is a rat here and let me show you what is going on." Taylor became privy to the secret.

On February 25, with all eyes on the Mecham trial, set to begin four days later, the Senate nonchalantly passed Bill 1188 and sent it over to the House. There it sat in Larry Hawke's committee while the Senate put Evan Mecham on trial. So far, everything was working just as the cave supporters had planned.

The trial of Mecham before the Arizona Senate was a painful and sometimes tumultuous one, presided over by Francis X. Gordon, chief justice of the Arizona Supreme Court. The proceedings went on for five weeks; Mecham himself testified over three days. Even as the trial was taking place, Republican leaders were gathering in secret to persuade Mecham to resign; they were unsuccessful. On the day the Senate was to make its decision, three hundred of the governor's supporters gathered outside the Capitol for a mock funeral, carrying a coffin labeled "The Arizona Constitution." Finally, on April 4, 1988, by votes of 21 to 9 and 26 to 4, the Arizona Senate found Governor Evan Mecham guilty

Columns and soda straws
in the Shelf Passage
(K. L. Day, Arizona
State Parks)

of "high crimes and misdemeanors" on two of the three articles of impeachment. He was the first sitting governor to be impeached in the United States in sixty years. Secretary of State Rose Mofford, a Democrat, was sworn in as the state's new (and first female) governor. The very morning after Mofford ascended to the governor's chair, Travous set up an appointment with her. They spent forty minutes together, and Travous told her about the cave, the "vehicle" bill, and everything that was going on. The new governor was pleased and enthusiastic.

Meanwhile, the legislative strategy and language, designed by Lane, Hawke, and Hays, was ready to move forward. Within the next few weeks, the plan was that the bill, which had already passed the Senate and was now sitting in Larry Hawke's House committee, would move out of committee to a vote of the full House, where it would be approved without a problem. Before that, some minor technical language would be changed in the House committee, making it different from the Senate bill; as a result, the Senate's John Hays would refuse to concur. A Senate-House "free" conference committee would then be appointed to reconcile the differences. The conference committee, according to plan, would add the language stating that donations and income derived from user and concession fees at other state parks "shall be segregated in a separate account within the state parks acquisition and development fund for the purchase and development of the property known as the J.A.K. property." J.A.K. stood for James A. Kartchner.

According to the legislation, this income from other state parks would continue to go to the cave until the purchase and development of the property was complete. In other words, the legislation put no restrictions of time or money on to the development of the cave—it gave State Parks practically a "blank check" for the J.A.K. property.

Once Bill 1188 was amended in this manner, it would go back to the House and Senate for approval and then to the governor for signing.

Things were getting close to a final vote—and public revelation. Then, weirdness happened. At four o'clock on a Friday, April 22, Travous received a call from Pat Kossan, a reporter for the (now defunct) *Phoenix Gazette,* the capital's afternoon daily and the state's second-largest newspaper.

"I want to know about your cave," she said, without stopping for small talk.

"What cave?" asked Travous, feigning innocence.

"I know all about it," she confided.

"You talk and I'll listen," said Travous.

Someone had clearly leaked the story to the *Gazette.* Kossan knew everything except the exact location of the cave. Her newspaper was going with the story the next day, she informed Travous. If that happened, the entire legislative strategy would be unmasked and Senate Bill 1188 might be killed. Travous grabbed a video that had recently been made of the cave and rushed over to the offices of the *Arizona Republic*. There he met with Bill Shover, the director of public affairs at Phoenix Newspapers, which operated both the *Republic* and *Gazette*. He told Shover the whole story. "But Pat doesn't work here," Shover informed him. "She works for the *Gazette*." What Travous didn't realize—he was relatively new to Arizona—was that the *Republic* and the *Gazette* were under joint ownership but not under joint editorial control; they were essentially rivals, each trying to outdo the other. "I had just spilled the whole story to the other paper!" Travous realized.

The mortified State Parks executive director then headed downstairs to meet with the editors of the *Gazette*. While Shover at the *Republic* had been sympathetic, that wasn't the case with the editors at its sister paper. Of the two papers, the *Gazette* was the smaller and the scrappier one. It had a scoop and was ready to go with it.

"We're in the business of news and this is news!" one of the editors proclaimed.

At that point, Travous lost his temper. "If this gets out and the cave is not protected, I'm going to make it known that you let it out!" he said. "I'm holding you responsible for this." It was as tough as he ever got.

There was silence in the room. A top editor asked, "How much time do you need?"

"How much time can you give me?" Travous asked.

"We'll give you a week," the editor said.

What the *Gazette* editors didn't know was that Travous had already promised an exclusive to Channel 3 Television News in Phoenix, which the previous month had put together a video about the cave for use in persuading legislators.

While Travous was facing down the newspaper editors, a flurry of phone calls took place between his deputy, Courtland Nelson, and Speaker Lane, and between Speaker Lane and the governor, who was rushing off to a speaking engagement in Tucson. Things were picking up speed. That evening, Dick Ferdon, the manager at the state park at Picacho Peak (the Civil War battle site northwest of Tucson where Confederate forces fended off an attack by Union soldiers in 1862) received a call from a high-ranking State Parks official. There was some "valuable property" that Arizona State Parks was looking at. Could Ferdon drop everything to watch the property for a month?

Ferdon was given directions to a designated milepost of State Highway 90 south of Benson where he was to be at 8 the next morning. There was a gate there, and he was to meet someone named Max. He was not to wear a uniform so as not to tip anyone off. Right before he left, he received word that he would be watching a cave. Max turned out to be Max Kartchner. What was supposed to be a one-month assignment turned out to be eleven months.

"It was just a hole in the ground," Ferdon remembers. "There were sensors inside. The alarm was powered by solar. It was so sensitive that every packrat who came along could set it off."

By Monday, April 25, everyone was racing against time. The word was obviously very close to getting out. The earliest that the legislation could go to both houses for final passage was Wednesday, the 27th. On Monday, the House passed an amended version of the bill, amended just enough so that the following day the Senate refused to concur, requiring the establishment of a conference committee. When some members questioned the amendment that Hawke made to the bill to make it different from the Senate's, he had replied, "Do it because I said so! This is something the Speaker wants out."

On Tuesday, whatever control that Travous, Lane, and Hawke had over the situation was deteriorating further. The *Gazette* had learned about Channel 3's exclusive video; the newspaper also knew the bill number and noticed in the legislative record that it would be taken up by both houses the following day. The editors were determined to publish their story without delay. The *San Pedro Valley News–Sun* in Benson also had the story and was ready to go with it in its weekly edition the next day; its reporter had interviewed members of the Kartchner family who, convinced it was pointless to try and suppress the story any longer, showed her some photos of the cave. Once it was clear that the *Gazette* would not hold off any longer, Travous granted Channel 3 permission to show its video that evening on its 10 o'clock news, even though the final votes had not been taken. At least the cave itself was protected at this point—Dick Ferdon was standing guard, with a gun holster on his belt.

Now, the moment had arrived to expand the "circle of confidence" from a few members to the entire legislature. Early that evening, Tuesday, Travous arrived at the Senate caucus. All reporters were asked to leave. He described the cave briefly, and all the senators marched over to Senate President Kunasek's office where they watched the still-under-wraps Channel 3 video. Coincidentally, Supreme Court Chief Justice Gordon, fresh from presiding over the Mecham trial, was paying a call on the legislature that day, as he did once a year. He was invited to watch the video along with the senators. "Mr. Chief Justice," Kunasek assured him, "this is not the way we normally conduct business."

The next morning, Wednesday, April 27, 1988, Randy Tufts and Gary Tenen headed for Phoenix and the Capitol building. It was the day of decision. The two were anxious—the Senate was considering a controversial piece of abortion legislation as well that day. Would that somehow delay Senate Bill 1188? Once they reached the State Parks office, they found a photographer from the *Gazette* waiting to take their picture. Copies of that day's newspaper lay on the table. The headline danced before their disbelieving eyes: "Fairy Tale Cave to Become Arizona's 25th State Park."

After lunch, as activists on both sides of the abortion issue streamed through the Capitol, shouting and waving placards, Travous went before the House caucus and explained all about "Secret Cave." The House appointed its representatives to the conference committee to work out differences between the House and Senate versions; they were Joe Lane, Larry Hawke, and Gus Arzberger, another legislator who represented Cochise County. All were passionate supporters of the cave. Senate conferees included John Hays, A. V. "Bill" Hardt, and Carol McDonald. Because the entire matter was pre-cooked, the committee members didn't even need to meet; their report, with the added language, was already prepared and was quickly sent to both the Senate and House. It included "emergency" language to make the legislation immediately operative in order to forestall any danger to the cave once the news was out. That afternoon, the Senate voted in favor of Bill 1188—this time including mention of the J.A.K. property—by 27–0. Tufts and Tenen, with Dean Kartchner next to them and other Kartchners present, sat in the gallery and watched the proceedings. The legislators gave them a standing ovation. When Tufts and Tenen were introduced, one senator was heard to say, "No wonder they found it. One of them's short and one of them's skinny."

In the House, however, there was one last moment of nervousness. When it came time to vote, a slew of "no" votes began to appear in the form of red lights on the chamber's electronic vote panel. The spectators were mystified. What was going on? The idea apparently was to play a trick on Lane, after all the members had gone through during impeachment and having been kept "out of the loop" on the cave. "Folks, it's the silly season," said Lane. They then changed their votes, and the bill went through 52–4. The dissenting votes were all protests related to the abortion legislation. It all happened so quickly that it was never necessary for The Nature Conservancy to acquire the property, even though the organization was prepared to do so.

Meanwhile, at 4:30 that afternoon, Governor Mofford was waiting to sign the bill in her office on the ninth floor of the Capitol. A large crowd assembled, including Tufts, Tenen, and the Kartchners. When the governor, known for her white beehive hairdo, tried to don a caver's hard hat and carbide lamp, the arrangement fell off her head to general hilarity. Even so, it marked the first major event of her administration and a chance for the state to "feel good" after the rancor and divisiveness of impeachment.

In the end, despite a few shaky moments, the acquisition of the cave had been approved exactly according to the plan devised by Travous, Lane, Hawke, and others several months before. Travous was a "master of the legislative process," in Gary Tenen's words; Joe Lane believed the State Parks agency director deserved "a hero medal" for his work. Still, there had been no public say or participation in the purchase of Kartchner. Even the media, usually so critical of governmental secrecy, felt that the ends justified the means in this case. "Ordinarily I would have been opposed to how it was done," said John Kromko, Tufts and Tenen's friend who had accompanied the pair on Tenen's first caving trip and who was a member of the Arizona House at the time. "But I understood they had to do it in secret. But had I not known Randy and trusted him, I would have blown the whistle on this." Added Tucson caver Steve Holland, "It was essentially a backroom deal and it could have backfired." But it didn't backfire. The "circle of confidence" so important to the cave had prevailed until almost the last moment; two very different kinds of secrecy—legislative and environmental—had coalesced to result in the preservation of the cave.

Surprisingly, impeachment, which could have derailed the legislation in a divided and preoccupied legislature, actually worked in the bill's favor, keeping legislators from "smelling a rat" and paying attention to the details, and potential pitfalls, of the acquisition. "If there had been anything other than impeachment going on and people focused on this, there could have been problems," said Lane. "Impeachment was a distraction. They [legislators] could have come up and said, 'Prove it to us. Tell us how much it will cost, what we will get, show us pictures, make this deal transparent.' But they didn't. If the thing had to stand on its own without anything to distract attention, I'm not sure it would have passed." For Lane, the cave was his swan song. His role in the impeachment process ended his political career that fall when he was narrowly defeated in a Republican primary in a district where as many as 40 percent of Republican voters were Mormons, many of them staunch Mecham supporters who blamed Lane for their hero's fall.

Travous saw it all in more cosmic terms. "It appears to me now that the stars were all lined up for this to happen," he said. "It was like a play that had already been written. Every time the plot needed to be moved along with another actor coming on stage, that person was there and they stepped on to the stage and kept it going.

"I was that person at one point, but others lined up too. It so happened that the head of the Senate Natural Resources Committee [John

Lois Kartchner (left), her son Max, and Arizona Governor Rose Mofford examine the cave photo that Mrs. Kartchner had kept out of sight for many years until the state bought the property (Kartchner family)

Hays] had been on the board of The Nature Conservancy and what looked to be an impossible time to get legislation passed—the Mecham impeachment—ended up being a great time to get legislation passed."

By the end of that day, Tufts and Tenen were elated. Tenen immediately telephoned his wife Judy. "Well, it's done!" he told her. The two men experienced many of the same feelings of euphoria as when they had first discovered the cave on that overcast day in November, nearly fourteen years before. "Then, we had achieved a goal—our goal of discovery," Tenen said. "Now, we had achieved a new goal."

That evening in Phoenix, at the Oaxaca Restaurant, a favorite gathering place for politicians and journalists, Tufts and Tenen joined State Parks staffers and their wives for a celebratory dinner. The mood was festive and relaxed. Representative Larry Hawke, so instrumental in the passage of Bill 1188, dropped by and told the cave discoverers, "I want you guys to find a cave in my district now. Hawke Caverns." Actually, this would be Tucson's state representative's last term; he was leaving the legislature to go to law school. The television over the bar, tuned to a local news channel, was reporting, "A fabulous secret cave was voted on today." Everyone cheered and ordered more beer. When the enchiladas arrived, Arizona State Parks Executive Director Travous leaned back in his chair and joked, "This is as good as it ever gets for a bureaucrat."

Meanwhile, at "Secret Cave," now known as Kartchner Caverns, Dick Ferdon wore his State Parks agency uniform for the first time since he had arrived five days earlier. His trailer was delivered the same day, so he could now sleep at the cave site, instead of at a Benson motel. The next morning, as he sat on the hill above the cave, he could see a line of cars all the way down the highway, trying to determine the location of the cave. "No one figured out that the cave was underground and they weren't going to see it anyway," he quipped. In nearby St. David, Lois Kartchner, widow of James A. Kartchner, removed from her bedroom wall a photograph that had been taken of the cave almost ten years before. It had been kept out of sight, in case visitors asked questions. Now, she proudly placed it on the wall in the living room for all to see.

And in Tucson, Randy Tufts and Gary Tenen were back home, feeling slightly dazed by the speed with which it had all happened. At Tenen's printing business, there was a constant barrage of media calls—"Gary on line 2. It's CBS!" At last, the secret that they had held so tightly and so passionately for fourteen years became known to the world. The two cavers experienced a tremendous sense of relief. "We could finally tell people about it," said Tenen. "We could finally tell our kids—kids can't keep secrets. It was exciting to talk about it and to hear it talked about."

All that Tufts and Tenen had worked toward was about to become reality. But now came the next challenge—how to develop a pristine, living cave into a world-class state park. It was a challenge that would turn out to be far more complex and would take many more years than anyone had expected.

TEN

From Desert Outpost to State Park

WHEN JIM WHITE, the cowboy who discovered New Mexico's Carlsbad Caverns, developed the cave for tourists in the early 1920s, he functioned as engineer, trail designer, construction boss, and crew. Working alone, he moved rocks and leveled passageways. He hammered discarded Ford automobile axles into crevices and strung galvanized wire between them for use as handholds, making it possible to cross the most perilous spots. The first visitors were transported 180 feet underground in an old guano bucket—two people could ride in it at one time, standing up. Carlsbad's first cave mapper, Willis T. Lee of the U.S. Geological Survey, relied on a ball of twine to avoid getting lost; he would unroll it behind him as he would enter a passageway. Eventually, White replaced the guano bucket with a wooden staircase. And once Calvin Coolidge established Carlsbad Caverns as a national monument, diesel engines and generators and floodlights were installed, to say nothing of a seven-hundred-seat lunchroom deep in the heart of the cave. By 1931, elevators were taking visitors down 754 feet to the Big Room, Carlsbad's largest chamber.

The effort to make Kartchner Caverns accessible to the public proved a far more complex process. Unlike Carlsbad, which is approximately 5 percent alive today, Kartchner is almost entirely a wet, "living" cave; it is also much smaller than its New Mexico counterpart, whose vast size could conceal most major mistakes or environmental damage. Kartchner's challenge, in both engineering and environmental terms, was daunting: how to create a tourist attraction in a cave whose major appeal lies in its pristine quality, where the speleothems are still growing, where an inadvertent movement, either during the development of the cave or after the arrival of tourists, could destroy some of the life and special character of the place, and where even seemingly slight changes in temperature and humidity could have permanently harmful effects.

Arizona State Parks was determined to avoid the mistakes in development that had occurred in Carlsbad and other caves around the country. At Kartchner there would be no floodlights—today, scientists have learned that lighting can raise temperatures and thus cause algae growth in the sensitive cave microclimate—and no food courts, with their proclivity to create fungus and bacteria and attract surface varmints. (At Carlsbad, non-native raccoons were rampant in the lunchroom area in the 1970s and '80s; an effort by the National Park Service and caving organizations to shut down the lunchroom on environmental grounds failed in 1994 after objections from New Mexico's congressional delegation.) There would be no stalagmite pipe organs playing "Oh Shenandoah," as at Virginia's Luray Caverns; no parking lot constructed right above the cave, as at Arkansas's Blanchard Springs Caverns.

"Everything was built with the idea of having one chance to do it right," said Jay Ream, Arizona State Parks regional manager in the 1990s (and later the agency's assistant director of parks), who was a member of the three-person team in charge of the day-to-day development of the cave. "We couldn't blame anyone else."

Long before the first tunnel was dug or the first trail was laid out, State Parks was planning pre-development studies to make Kartchner Caverns the best-studied cave in America, if not the world. To facilitate this, even before the state officially purchased the cave from the Kartchner family in September 1988, Tufts, Tenen, and other local cavers established a nonprofit organization called Arizona Conservation Projects, Inc. (ACPI). Secrecy remained a concern at this point: the organization's title did not include the word "cave." Despite the participation of the two cave discoverers, ACPI was required to participate in a bidding process for the contract to do the pre-development studies, just like any other ordinary consulting company.

Tufts and Tenen recruited a host of caving experts from around the country as advisers. Ron Bridgemon, who was running Arizona's state crime lab in Tucson at the time and serving as the president of the Cave Research Foundation, an organization that does scientific studies around the country, was named president of ACPI's board. Tucson caver Bob Buecher became the project manager; he and Tufts would be ACPI's only full-time paid employees. It was an impressive lineup in terms of caving knowledge and brainpower, helped considerably by

Setting a lead wire for the infrared camera for the first bat studies (Arizona State Parks)

Bridgemon's and Buecher's reputations and by contract work for government agencies previously done by the Cave Research Foundation and individuals associated with it. Despite its lack of track record as an organization, ACPI outbid five commercial environmental-assessment companies for the contract. The amount of the contract for the entire process was $453,736; the plan called for underground pre-development studies to be completed within two years, and assuming that all went smoothly, the new state park would open to the public in 1994.

Things got off to a promising start. The Arizona caving community mobilized, with some fifty to sixty cavers working as ACPI volunteers. In its first year, ACPI brought in geologists, hydrologists, and mineralogists to map the cave and to establish baselines to measure potential effects of development. Twenty-two environmental monitoring stations were set up to measure rates of temperature, humidity, and evaporation and to monitor the impact of proposed entrances on the cave's microclimate. Paleontologists searched for fossils, finding the skeleton of a thirty-four-thousand-year-old horse and determining that the eighty-thousand-year-old bones of what had been thought to be a bison were actually those of a sloth. Cave biologists studied plants and animals, notably the *Myotis velifer* bats that roosted in summer on the ceiling in the Big Room.

In some 375 visits to the cave, ACPI could claim a host of achievements in understanding everything from radon levels (visitors to the cave would experience less than 1/10 of the accepted guideline for public exposure to radioactivity) to the age of cave formations (ranging from 40,000 to almost 200,000 years) to bat biology (ACPI's final report proposed that visitation to the Big Room be restricted during May to mid-September so as not to disturb the bats).

But a personality conflict between Tufts and Buecher slowed progress. Buecher was a Rhode Island–born civil engineer who had come out to Tucson in 1967 to go to the University of Arizona. A few years later, while caving, he met his wife Debbie; the two became active in cave rescue operations in Arizona, and Bob emerged as an important player in various aspects of Kartchner exploration and research starting in the mid-1980s. Bob Buecher probably knew more about caves than anyone in the state of Arizona. But he also had difficulty getting along with colleagues—he could be uncommunicative and had a hard time tolerating opinions that differed from his own—according to various individuals involved with ACPI; at the same time, Tufts's penchant for analysis, which had frustrated even his friend Gary Tenen at times, thoroughly exasperated Buecher.

"When we first started, we discovered we could not work together," said Buecher. "There was a clash of philosophies. I am an engineer—

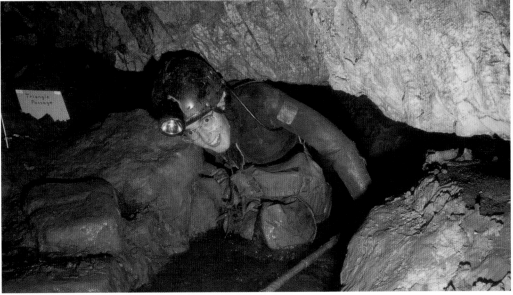

engineers solve problems. Randy was more of a philosopher." To Buecher, Tufts would "wake up every morning and rebuild the universe from scratch. With me, with my engineering background, it would be 'OK, we made this decision and this is the direction are going in.' But the next morning Randy would be recreating his universe, thinking, 'Wait a minute, maybe we should be doing this.'"

By January 1991—more than two years into the pre-development process—the conflict had taken its toll. In a letter to Steve Holland, ACPI board president at the time, Tufts wrote that he was resigning

Bob Buecher, project manager for Kartchner's pre-development studies, navigates his way to the Big Room (K. L. Day, Arizona State Parks)

Debbie Buecher, caver and bat scientist (Bob Buecher)

from the board of directors. "The communications problems evident at the end of our 11/14/90 Board meeting have led me to conclude that I no longer exercise meaningful influence over the actions of our Project Manager Bob Buecher," he wrote. "At the same time it is probably too late to make the internal administrative changes that might remedy the situation . . . I nevertheless can no longer remain a board member attesting to project management actions over which I have ceased to have control." Although that particular letter was apparently never sent, Tufts and most of the other prominent cavers in ACPI departed, leaving Buecher to complete the pre-development studies with the help of a handful of volunteers.

In January 1992, after more than three years of work on what was supposed to be a two-year project, Buecher and what was left of ACPI submitted a 365-page exhaustive document of studies and recommendations, many of which provided the intellectual basis for the development to follow. But, by that point, longtime friendships had been frayed. "Buecher completed the project, but the checks and balances were gone," said Rafael Payan, the development director for Arizona State Parks at the time. "It was scary for us at State Parks. We knew that Bob Buecher was a great scientist, but he didn't have the checks and balances." Payan, today the director of Pima County's [Tucson] Natural Resources, Parks & Recreation Department, was one of the triumvirate in charge of development, along with Ream and, starting in 1995, Project Manager Bob Burnett.

While ACPI was doing research inside the cave, aboveground, State Parks officials were formulating the basic outlines of the new park. "We were figuring out things like how many toilets do we need," said Jeff Dexter, who became park manager as of June 1989 after stints at Arizona's Yuma Crossing and Roper Lake state parks. "To do that, we had to figure out how many visitors would come and how long would they stay. How many cars would be in the parking lot? When would they show up and how long would they stay? There was a lot of number-crunching and guessing that went on at this stage."

Meanwhile, Tufts, Tenen, and State Parks officials were tossing around various ideas—sometimes wildly adventuresome ones—about how to open the cave to the public in a way that would provide maximum environmental protection. One idea, according to Payan, involved cutting holes in the hillsides surrounding Kartchner and creating sealed, glass-enclosed vestibules for viewing; that would keep the visitors outside of the cave per se but would enable them to have a good look into it. But Tufts opposed this notion, arguing that it would provide little difference from a photograph; he wanted visitors to have a sensory experience of the cave, to smell and feel it. Another proposal

Jeff Dexter, first Kartchner Caverns State Park manager, in the Strawberry Room (Bob Buecher)

centered around the creation of small glass decks or porticos within the cave, allowing visitors inside but again keeping them at a distance. The trouble was that the visitor's view of the cave would be marred by visible glass tubing, and the plan also raised issues about the cave's perpetually dripping water knocking on the glass. Yet another idea suggested constructing more conventional trails and ramps outside the cave and then using a forklift to bring them inside (workers would be airlifted into the cave as well—perhaps by helicopter). This would protect the cave floor and formations as much as possible. But the technology wasn't advanced enough for this approach, and no one could be absolutely positive whether ramps and trails created outside the cave would match up exactly with the interior dimensions anyway.

One of the problems was that few people knew how to build underground. "The last big cave jobs were twenty and thirty years before, and the guys who had done them were now in their 70s and 80s," said Dexter. "We had a couple of them on our advisory board. One died and another had open-heart surgery." The project manager at Blanchard Springs in Arkansas, which opened to the public in 1973, was quite elderly and unable to travel; State Parks officials went and visited him.

So State Parks relied on experts who Tufts and Tenen had consulted in the early days after the cave's discovery: Orion Knox, who had first mapped Xanadu and who had helped discover and develop Natural Bridge Caverns in Texas in the early 1960s; Jack Burch, who had developed Caverns of Sonora, where Gary Tenen had learned to construct trails; and Jeanne and Russell Gurnee, whose ideas on cave commercialization had inspired Tufts and Tenen more than a decade before. "They said, 'Why not do it the old-fashioned way but do it very carefully—make it linear and tight and protect air flows,'" recalled Payan. "It had been done before. And we could cost it out. The other ideas had never been done before, and so we were unable to estimate the costs."

Finally, it was decided. Tunnels, not staircases or elevators, would take visitors into the cave, where they would walk along some 1,200 feet of ramped, raised trails, all following state-of-the-art environmental safeguards. This possessed the added advantage of making the cave accessible to people with disabilities. Entrances and tunnels would be constructed at the same level as the sinkhole, in order to make sure that air wouldn't leave the cave in a kind of "chimney effect," disrupting the fragile microclimate. Large airlock doors—similar to those used in a meat-packing freezer—would lead into the entrance to the tunnels, again with the aim of keeping the humid cave air in and the dry outside air out. "Much of our decision to put in horizontal tunnels and airlocks came from the National Park experience at Carlsbad Caverns," said Rick Toomey, the scientist who served as cave resources manager (later science and research manager) for Arizona State Parks from April 2001 to May 2005. "Elevators caused incredible evaporation and drying out of the Big Room in Carlsbad. There used to be extensive pools at Carlsbad and they evaporated within ten years. Pools don't regenerate. They figured out what happened and put an airlock in there but it was too late."

Before construction could begin, there were other matters to attend to—the creation of infrastructure, for starters. Although it was close to a highway and not far from two decent-sized towns, Benson and Sierra Vista, Kartchner Caverns might as well have been in the middle of nowhere. For the first year after the state acquired the property, the only thing that was visible was Dick Ferdon's trailer, parked near where the Discovery Center sits today. Roads had to be built to the site itself and utilities brought in. There was nothing—no water, no sewer, no electrical, no telephone. "It was extremely primitive," said Park Manager Dexter. "The road was horrendous. There was no sign of civilization. It was a desert outpost. Utilities were ten miles away. We worked out of town [Benson] just to be able to answer the phone. Finally, we got a clunky cell phone that worked." But during his early days there, Dexter says, "When I was at the site or in the cave, I was outside of the agency's communications."

When negotiations with the local power company to bring electricity from the interstate to the cave area proved unsuccessful, State Parks built its own power lines, eight miles of them, at significantly less cost than what the power company had proposed. Eventually, Kartchner would have its own electric lines, its own sewer-treatment plant, and its own water system. However, it would be years, until May 1997, until a landline telephone system was up and running.

Meanwhile, nothing was happening on schedule. The pre-development studies had continued far longer than anticipated. The creation of infrastructure proved more complicated than anyone had thought. Major rainstorms and flooding hit Arizona, and State Parks officials, worried about the instability of the sinkhole and the initial crawlways, put the entrance area off-limits. There was suddenly no way in or out. In the fall of 1994, State Parks drilled a forty-four-foot shaft—essentially a vertical stairway with ladders and steel landings—at the top of the hill to gain entry. The shaft offered major advantages over the cramped access of the original entrance because workmen could now move big, bulky materials into the cave, something which had been previously impossible. Still, it was obvious that the original 1994 target date couldn't possibly be met; by the time 1994 rolled around, the date for the opening was moved to the fall of 1997.

Financial ups and downs played a part in the delays as well. The new state park was being created "paycheck to paycheck," as Ream put it. Senate Bill 1188, passed with so little scrutiny during the impeachment period, had established an Acquisition and Development (A&D) fund that gave Kartchner the ability to finance its development through user and concession fees collected by other state parks, with no end-date specified. This was good for Kartchner, obviously, but not necessarily for other state parks. With their revenues going to Kartchner, the other parks were being drained of financial resources needed to perform maintenance and make improvements; "Kartchner envy" was widespread. Then, in 1991, the state of Arizona experienced a financial crisis. To cope with revenue shortfalls, state officials slashed some $1 million from general fund monies used to support State Parks operations. With operations money cut in half, the agency had to make up the loss somehow, lest it be forced to close down a number of facilities. As a result, State Parks officials were forced to take $1 million or so a year in user fees slated to go to the A&D fund for Kartchner development and use them to cover operations instead. Suddenly, Kartchner was staring at the loss of a million dollars a year.

This situation was further complicated when, at about the same time, Arizona State Parks purchased Tonto Natural Bridge, the largest natural travertine (Italianate limestone) bridge in the world, located near

Payson, northeast of Phoenix. State Parks had had its eye on Tonto since the 1950s but had been stymied by legal difficulties. With the state suffering from financial problems, the only way for State Parks to acquire Tonto was to tap the A&D fund yet again. The purchase agreement for Tonto involved taking $350,000 out of the fund each year over 20 years. That meant another chunk of parks revenues intended for Kartchner development went instead to pay for the Tonto acquisition.

Fortunately, other funding sources were available to keep work on the cave going. The Arizona Department of Transportation paid for the road projects within the new park grounds, as well as the road up to the cave and the parking lot. That came to $3.5 million. And in 1990, in a move that was to prove crucial for Kartchner, the state's voters approved an initiative establishing the Heritage Fund—the brainchild of The Nature Conservancy—under which Arizona State Parks and the state's Game and Fish Department would each receive $10 million every year from state lottery revenues. Up to 35 percent of State Parks's $10-million share was eligible to be spent at Kartchner, guaranteeing a continuing revenue stream.

Meanwhile, the planning for the construction of the first underground project—the entry tunnels leading into the cave—was going forward; construction inside the cave could not begin until the tunnels were largely completed. The route would not go through the sinkhole, which was perceived as far too unstable. Instead, the entrance would be created farther toward the northern side of the hill. Although the tunnels were outside the cave proper, State Parks officials still worried about using dynamite; they were concerned that the particle velocity of the blasts in the tunnels might harm the cave itself, particularly the fragile 21.2-foot soda straw, ranked as the second-longest known soda straw in the world. So, the managers explored using a high-pressure water cannon—a kind of giant squirt gun—to cut the tunnels through the limestone face of the hill. The idea was "like turning on a water hose full blast and digging a hole in the ground," said Ream. "You would use water jets to cut slots in the rock and then take hydraulic splitters and break in between the slots and muck everything out." The concept sounded intriguing, and the water cannon arrived from St. Louis at great expense. But after a year of trying to develop the technology to suit the needs at Kartchner, State Parks gave up: the limestone turned out to be simply too hard. The water failed to cut the rock, even when little pieces of steel were inserted in the water. "There was water everywhere," said Ream. "The miners were going nuts. So we backed off the technology and finally used dynamite." It had been a costly and time-consuming experiment.

A soft pipe attached to a blower brings fresh air to the end of a tunnel where miners were working (Arizona State Parks)

A mucker, which was used to remove rock after the rock was blasted out with dynamite or broken up with jackhammers (Arizona State Parks)

Finally, by the summer of 1995—a year after the park was supposed to be opened—the tunneling began. The plan was for 1,100 feet of entry tunnels ten to fourteen feet wide and high; a mining company out of Prescott, in northern Arizona, was hired to do the job, using standard mining production equipment—jack leg drills (rock drills) and muckers (long, low trucks with a bucket to remove debris). The tunnels were made wide enough to accommodate conventional mining equipment—State Parks viewed this phase, first and foremost, as a mining/engineering project—which may have made the tunnels unnecessarily large, at least in the view of some cavers. It was a decision that would also be criticized after the fact for perhaps allowing outside air to enter the cave, creating a drying effect within.

The procedure was relatively straightforward. Miners would drill holes, from four to six feet in depth and about one and a half inches in diameter, into the face of the rock, packing the holes with dynamite. In a concession to concerns about possible damage to the cave itself,

Drilling holes for dynamiting
(Arizona State Parks)

they used dynamite charges much lower than usually employed in mining—in this case, two pounds of dynamite for a four-foot hole and three pounds for a six-foot hole. The charges were set, and everyone would leave the hill. The dynamite-filled holes would explode first, creating a cavity. As the explosions continued, the cavity was enlarged. In addition to the relatively low charges, only two holes were blasted at a time, moving from left to right, in order to reduce vibration in the cave. The mining official in charge of the blasting was constantly tinkering with the blasting sequences, trying to get the maximum effect with minimum potential damage.

During the test blasts some months before, Park Manager Dexter had ensconced himself inside the cave to see if any harm was done to the delicate underground formations from the dynamite; the formations were untouched, but for Dexter himself it proved a daunting experience, like "sitting underground while they were shooting explosives over my head," as he described it.

At first progress was good, and tunnel construction advanced at a rate of about six feet a day, sometimes more. However, before long the miners met difficulties. For one thing, they ran into fault lines that hadn't been expected. "One day we'd make ten feet but right behind there would be a major fault line and we'd have to go for months on end just a couple of feet a day," said Payan. This was particularly difficult during work on the Big Room tunnel. There the rock was so porous that sometimes miners could barely move forward at all as crumbling rock

Workmen installing a stabilizing column during the tunneling phase (Arizona State Parks)

collapsed all around them. It resembled a giant sand hill, and some days their progress was measured not in feet but in inches.

To create the exit tunnel from the Big Room, State Parks removed thousands of cubic feet of earth. "We had to rip out the whole side of the mountain, put a concrete tunnel in there, and then bring it back and re-vegetate it," said Payan. It was all like "remodeling an old house where you had never lived," he said. "Every time we looked and thought that we would have a solution, there was always a new twist to it." This approach to the Big Room tunnel proved controversial, dismaying some cavers, including Tufts and Tenen, who thought that "scraping the living daylights out of that hill," in Tenen's words, could have been avoided by using a lower-tech solution.

Meanwhile, miners were constantly leaving to work in the gold mines at Elko, in northern Nevada, where they could earn more money. The result was an ongoing drain of trained workers. And the reason wasn't just the pay scale. The compromises required to work in a fragile environment like Kartchner didn't sit well with many of the miners. "Miners like a twenty-foot boom," said Dexter, unlike at Kartchner where, out of concern for cave formations, the "booms" were only a modest four to six feet.

What was supposed to take nine months took two and a half years, straining State Parks's budgets. Finally, in the spring of 1997, the miners broke through into the cave. Some trail work inside had already started several months earlier, but construction within the cave could only take place on weekends because the tunnel blasting was going on during the week. It was nine years since the cave had been acquired from the Kartchner family, and nothing was open to the public yet.

For Gary Tenen and Randy Tufts, the 1990s proved a difficult period, when it came to the cave. They had a hard time letting go. "It was as if Randy and Gary were the parents, and we had just married their daughter," said State Parks Executive Director Travous. Rafael Payan continued the parent-child metaphor: it was as though Randy and Gary had given birth and had to hand over the baby. It wasn't that they were unhappy that Arizona State Parks was in charge, and they professed great faith in Ken Travous. Travous, in Tufts's view, was "a first-rate public servant, one of the best public administrators I have worked with."

The problem was just that the two discoverers were anxious about the cave—a lot of the time. As Tufts himself wrote in 1995, " . . . with less and less contact with the project I worry about it . . . Yet as I necessarily withdraw from involvement with it I rarely know how to act regarding the cave and the State Parks Dept. . . . While the cave has a good home, matters such as staff turnover and the need for cave expertise give me pause . . . The preoccupation never goes away."

As with any devoted parents, things were bothering Tufts and Tenen, false starts, sloppiness, minor mistakes—"nothing insurmountable," in Tufts's words—but also larger issues like the size of the tunnels. These matters particularly affected Tufts; the cave was his "only child," while Gary and Judy Tenen had three children of their own, plus the cave, of course. "So when I catch little snippets of difficulties at the cave, I worry," Tufts wrote. "How is it going? Should I act? Not act?" Tufts

Randy Tufts (right) visits the cave worksite (Gary Tenen)

would telephone Travous during the evening at home—even once at 4 a.m.—with various suggestions and concerns, many of them legitimate, many of them helpful, but the State Parks director wasn't getting much sleep.

In Travous's view, Tufts was too close to the project, in the emotional sense, and this was affecting the ability of State Parks officials to do their day-to-day job. He respected both Tufts and Tenen—after all, their conservation and stewardship ethic were the inspiration for State Parks's entire approach to cave development, and they knew virtually every stalagmite and stalactite in the cave—but they had to back off. He told the two discoverers they could no longer visit the cave when construction was going on. "We pretty much had to lock them out," recalled Jay Ream. "It is like when you drop your kid off at the first day of school. If you hang around, they are just going to cry longer. You really needed to let go. So they had to be locked out of it. They were impeding progress." For his part, Tenen insists that he was never banned from Kartchner. "My attitude was, 'State Parks bought it, it's theirs; it's time for us to butt out,'" he says. "But Randy kept a closer eye on stuff."

Not everyone perceived it exactly the same way. "Different people at State Parks wanted different levels of their involvement," said State Parks development director Rafael Payan. "I don't think Randy and Gary were involved enough. I wish they could have been there every day that we were doing something, certainly during the most critical stages. They weren't as engaged as I would have liked them to be, in retrospect."

Tufts, predictably, took a philosophical view. It made no sense, in his view, to believe that State Parks officials really knew what they were doing at Kartchner. How could they? "Think about it," Tufts wrote. "They have never done a cave before. . . . About the most you could do is to feel your way and hope for the best." No one had a monopoly on know-how as far as the cave was concerned. Almost anyone's suggestions might be valuable, he thought. With him and Tenen lessening their involvement, it was incumbent on the State Parks staff to speak up. "So what do you do when you realize you don't know what you're doing?" he asked. "You talk with the cave. What I mean is that the cave is the source of inspiration for the whole thing. The goal was not to create a park that just happened to have a cave. The goal was to protect the cave using the park as a vehicle. From the cave comes the inspiration to persist despite difficulty. The cave is the best guide."

He added, "If there is a question go to the cave . . . Talking with it, not to it. And as those involved grow in knowledge and love for this beautiful place, they may also talk with, not to, each other."

Five years before, in 1990, Tufts had returned to school as a graduate student in geosciences at the University of Arizona. In 1995, the same year he wrote those words, he joined a research group studying Europa, one of the moons of the planet Jupiter. He realized he needed to move on, and when the opportunity presented itself, he did so.

The construction of the tunnels was not the only thing happening at the new state park. Work began on the visitor center, called the Discovery Center, just across Guindani Wash from the cave, starting in August 1996. Although originally sentiment had existed for an inexpensive Quonset hut with a Kodak booth to take tickets, in the end State Parks officials decided to create a world-class visitor center, with permanent exhibits and a gift shop. Designed by the Scottsdale firm of Vernon Swaback, it would be 23,000 square feet in size and integrate the architecture of the building with the mountains behind it. As visitors entered, the building would get darker and darker, much like a cave. While the Discovery Center was going up, a crew was building a bridge across the wash leading to the cave, and a second crew was constructing maintenance facilities and the visitors' campground.

Meanwhile, Bruce Herschend, whose family had developed the Silver Dollar City theme park around Marvel (originally Marble) Cave in Branson, Missouri, was spending days in the cave, sketching out trails. He would sit for an hour in one spot, visualizing where a trail would go, where it would stop and start. Then he would move on to another location and do the same thing. It was the artist at work. Herschend believed that, when feasible, the trails should go along the same paths that the discoverers had taken. His plan to make the trails accessible to people with disabilities would be the first time ever in a show cave in the United States.

In April 1997, the miners had broken through to the cave itself. The last stages had been accomplished with extreme caution: workers used barriers made up of mattresses and railroad ties with plastic behind them to prevent shards of rock from falling into the cave proper; plastic sheets covered the work zone, creating a particularly uncomfortable work environment in such a humid area. Now, it was time to start making the interior portions of the cave accessible to the public. The Rotunda and Throne rooms complex, which included the Kubla Khan formation and the 21.2-foot soda straw, would come first. With State Parks under pressure to show some results, it made sense to do the most spectacular chamber first. The Big Room would be developed later, after the Rotunda-Throne complex was open to the public, even though the access tunnels to the chamber were already completed.

If there was a certain amount of leeway given to miners in building the tunnels—in many ways, theirs had been just an ordinary, if difficult, tunneling job—that vanished almost entirely once work started within the cave itself. Development was now taking place inside Xanadu, in that vulnerable and timeless realm, where the water was still dripping and seeping and breathing life into cave formations that had been undisturbed for thousands of years. "Once those tunnels stopped and the cave began, it wasn't a mine anymore," said Ream.

Arizona State Parks officials permitted vehicles through the tunnels up to the entrance of the cave, but no farther. After that, everything—concrete, rock, wire—had to be hauled in by wheelbarrow or in five-gallon buckets. In order to protect the cave environment, work crews used only hand tools; the only power tools allowed were hydraulic hammer drills and electric saws with carbide blades. There was a danger that lubricants could leak and get into the cave, and the moist environment was hard on tools as well; for these reasons, much of the equipment had to be removed every night. Gas-powered tools that could create fumes or spill oil were banned. No welding was allowed within the cave either. And workers had to bring out all debris, not dump it in corners as Gary Tenen had observed at the Caverns of Sonora.

As Dave Irwin noted in an article in the *Tucson Weekly,* "Developing the cave is akin to capturing King Kong, and rather than plopping him on a stage, you take his natural ecosystem, and unobtrusively build fully

Crew member (and later tour guide) Chuck Duncan wheels a load of concrete into the cave during trail construction. Most of the concrete was brought in by wheelbarrow and bucket. (Arizona State Parks)

wheelchair-accessible observation points for all the ape's activities and interesting body parts, while hoping he never notices you watching."

If miners had been employed to work on the tunnels, that wasn't going to be the case this time around. For the interior of the cave, State Parks was determined to use its own people—mostly park rangers and park employees, but former construction workers and some cavers as well. Many of them needed lessons in cave courtesy. "We took a group of construction workers who were used to working on the surface and taught them etiquette," said Ginger Nolan, now the head of Kartchner's cave unit, which specializes in monitoring and maintenance, who arrived there in February 1997 as cave environmentalist. "They were used to chewing tobacco, to eating while they were working. We had to change all of those rules. There was no spitting in the cave, and they had to wear gloves because oils from their skin would grow fungus on

THE MAKING OF KARTCHNER CAVERNS

the cave. We'd have a full day of training, and then at the end, we'd take them down the shaft."

Nolan notes that working on the trails at Kartchner was an economic boon for these workers in the relatively depressed area that was southeast Arizona. Still, "some of them would get into the cave and they just didn't hack it," she said. "It was just too overwhelming—very wet, very humid, very hot, especially when you're working."

The result was a "horrendous turnover" of employees working on the trailbuilding, according to Dexter. If one or two of a hiring group of six or seven remained after several months, that was considered a success. One of the reasons, he says, was that the work was so hard. Another factor was the humidity. Employees would be covered with moisture after only twenty minutes of work, and they would continue at their jobs, sopping wet, for another seven, eight, or ten hours. Everyone had to work at what was called the "cave's pace," said Dexter. You didn't want to exceed the cave's pace by working too hard because you would sweat too much; if you worked slower than the cave's pace, you would get cold. Workers fell ill, especially in winter, when they'd take breaks outside in forty-two-degree weather, while soaking wet.

During her first three weeks on the job, Nolan wondered if she was going to last at Kartchner. After each day of work, she'd go home, lie in the bathtub, and engage in deep breathing. "You got used to it," she said, "but it took a while."

Although her official job description was environmental monitoring, Nolan quickly found herself doing the same tasks as the rest of the fifty to sixty men and women working at Kartchner. "Everyone did whatever it took," she said. "We had a concrete pour—everyone lined up for concrete pour. We had a wire pull, and everyone lined up for wire pull. We were laying conduit, and everyone was there for the conduit. We worked very well as a team. It was a very exciting process."

There were always women working there, up to 35 percent of the fifty- to sixty-person crew at one point. "The women would do it all," said Nolan. "One of the best rock layers was a woman. The chief electrician was a woman. We were so buff!"

Before anything was done inside the cave, mock-ups took place outside. Workers did practice-building of trails outside the cave, in an effort to train people to stand within a very narrow space inside and not get in each other's way. "Everything we would do, we would do outside the cave and make sure we had it down pat before going inside," says Payan. "It was like what NASA did for their moon walks when they would practice on sand dunes."

Inside the cave, extra care had to be taken. It was crucial to contain hair and skin oils, if possible; perspiration had to be prevented from spattering on rocks, where it could result in bacteria and fungus. Another major concern was lint, perhaps the most intractable problem that caves in general face. Lint contains phosphates from detergents and can serve as fertilizer, promoting the growth of bacteria, fungus, and algae. It dropped off clothes every time pants rubbed together and could float hundreds of feet off the trail. "Everyone who goes into a cave leaves behind a belly button full of lint, skin cells, and dust," noted Tom Aley, owner and director of the Ozark Underground Laboratory in Protem, Missouri.

Each day, the construction crews at Kartchner Caverns would have their clothes misted—like vegetables in the local supermarket—in order to prevent tiny fibers of lint from falling from their clothes. At the very least, the misting assured that lint would drop straight down on the trail and not in the direction of the formations. Trails were designed with eighteen-inch-high curbs so that, once the cave opened to tourists, lint would not float off the trails; every night, workers hosed down the trails. This was another case of learning from the experience of other caves: at Carlsbad, over a twelve-year period, volunteers had removed 154 pounds of lint, and it has been a huge problem at caves like Kentucky's Mammoth and South Dakota's Wind Cave as well.

The work itself was deliberate, methodical, even tedious. On the day when the *Tucson Weekly's* Dave Irwin visited the cave, he reported that work "consisted of lugging 600 feet of 8-inch-high pressure hose into the cave in 20-foot sections, locking it all together, backing a concrete truck up and pumping cement to cover an 8-square-yard area of trail. Then workers flushed the hose and carried it back." The whole procedure took the crew about half the shift. "And this was a speedy procedure," he went on. "In many places, they have to carry the cement in wheelbarrows to the work site deep within the cave."

As on any construction job, there were endless unanticipated problems and difficulties, but these were intensified by working in a cave. Electric wire grew mold in the humid underground environment; State Parks had to buy a special kind of wire that was made only by a small company in Vermont. The lubricant in the telephone wire developed a mold problem too. A rock saw became obsolete midway through construction; the managers were unable to get parts. Then there was the problem of filters for a vacuum-cleaner component of some of the welding equipment. The construction crew ran out of filters, and State Parks officials discovered that they were manufactured only once a year in Sweden and that every U.S. supplier was out of them. When the filters were found on a computerized list in one warehouse, State Parks officials were jubilant; then they found out that the numbering system had been changed and no one could locate the filters. "There were adventures like that every day," said Dexter. "You seldom knew if you made the right decision. The easiest decision always came back to bite you."

At one point, a five-gallon bucket rolled off a slope and landed in the middle of the dramatic expanse of the mud floor of the Rotunda Room, where no human being had stepped for all eternity. Tufts and Tenen and State Parks had refused to allow anyone to walk on the pristine mud with its giant cracks; there had never been a footprint on it. Now there was a bucket sitting smack in the middle. As Rafael Payan tells the story, everyone was scratching their heads—what should be done? Rent a model helicopter? But the cave managers knew that the mud floor would eventually fill up with water. And so it did—during the summer monsoon rains almost a year later. "Once the water got high enough, we took the skinniest kid on the construction crew and put him on an air raft and floated him out there," recalled Payan. "He plucked the bucket very carefully and brought it back." In this way, the development crew preserved one of the most unique features of the cave.

In the early years of studies and construction, bureaucrats and state legislators generally kept out of the way. The delays and the costs may have raised eyebrows, but the money to develop Kartchner wasn't coming out of general revenues. Even before the tunnels were built, State Parks officials would accompany various legislators, wearing hard hats and knee pads, on visits to Kartchner. If the legislators arrived at the cave a little antsy—everyone wanted the cave opened during their term in office, to reflect well on them—after their visit, they were usually mollified. "The majority of the money to build the park came from Parks revenues, but certain legislative committees had to approve the release of the money," noted Jay Ziemann, now assistant parks director, who functioned as the agency's liaison to the legislature during this period and frequently accompanied legislators on tours. "So it was important to keep on good terms with them. The idea was to engage them in the cave." Ziemann says that the main problem wasn't really money; the cave and State Parks were generating enough of that. "It was the development [itself] that took time," he said. "The development and the number of people who could be working at Kartchner at one time were the limiting factors, rather than the money."

Equally important was the fact that, thanks to both the legislature and then-governor Fife Symington, Kartchner was exempted from portions of the state's procurement code, starting in April 1996. As a general rule, state construction is put out to bid. But in developing a cave, there were no clear guidelines, and State Parks officials argued successfully that it was impossible to have a reasonable competitive bidding process. "You develop a cave by 'yonders' and 'surelys,'" said Ziemann. "You want to go yonder and surely you can get there! But you can't engineer this. It isn't like putting a sidewalk in front of your house where you measure exactly the length and dimensions and choose the lowest bid. Developing a cave is different. You have no idea where a trail would go exactly. There are stability problems. It is so unique. And portions of the procurement code made it impossible to do this. In some cases we needed expertise and couldn't go with the lowest bid." Kartchner's exemption was renewed by the legislature in 1999 through the year 2002, extending through the completion of the development of the Big Room.

One official who tried to challenge the State Parks agency over Kartchner was Douglas K. Martin, the state's mine inspector. Arizona's mine inspector post is an elected one—the only such elected position in the country—and Martin had authority over health and safety in the tunnels at Kartchner. The tunnels were considered to be a mining project. But Martin, a flamboyant character known for dressing in cowboy regalia, was determined to extend his authority to the cave itself. In the northeast-central part of the Rotunda Room, there is a huge crack across the ceiling at the point where it slopes downward—two slabs formed by the intermittent collapse of rock layers thousands of years ago. Mine inspectors who were teaching the crews at Kartchner classes in underground safety took note of the ceiling and became alarmed, reporting back to their boss that it might be dangerous. State Parks officials countered that what appeared to be a crack in ceiling simply indicated a state of repose, "safer than the Empire State Building."

But the mine inspector was unconvinced. In October 1997, just as the construction of trails was about to begin, Martin called a meeting, attended by Ziemann, Payan, and twelve people from the mine inspector's office. The meeting was tense, with Martin upbraiding State Parks officials, telling them that the cave was unsafe; he wanted to install rock bolts in the cave ceiling. Arizona State Parks, fearing that Martin was trying to take control of the cave—and concerned that bolting the ceiling could make it less, not more stable—was determined to stop him.

Soon after, in early December, a meeting was held at the cave. Martin didn't attend, sending two of his deputies instead. Arizona State Parks Executive Director Travous was present. The governor's office sent Larry Agenbroad, a professor at Northern Arizona University (NAU), as an unbiased voice upon whom the governor could rely. J. Jackson Harper, a well-known geologist from Texas, was also in attendance. Agenbroad examined the situation, concluding that the rock was in equilibrium and there was little cause for concern. Harper, the geologist, took the same position; still, he suggested that it might be good to have certain gauges to take monthly readings of the stability. "You mean these things?" asked Travous, pointing to monitors that had already been installed. State Parks seemed to have an answer to every objection. Then, Travous invited everyone to tour the cave. At that point, as Dexter, who was present at the meeting, recalls, one of the mine inspection officials said, "If you don't do it our way, we'll walk." And they did. The mine inspector's office eventually abandoned any attempt to declare the cave unsafe. However, Martin's attempt to intervene underscored the complexity of the bureaucratic maneuvering that proved almost as crucial as the construction process itself. (In December 2006, a state grand jury indicted Martin on nine counts of fraud, theft, and violations of state purchasing procedures, involving thousands of dollars.)

By 1998, it had been almost ten years since State Parks acquired the "J.A.K. property," and Kartchner still wasn't open. After a period of relative patience, the legislature was getting frustrated; many of the cave's earliest supporters had long since departed. Even if Kartchner wasn't taking money out of the general revenues, it continued to gobble up more and more of State Parks user fees and Heritage Fund monies. It was a "motherhood" project, in many ways, as Tufts noted, but it was also becoming "Nature's Money Pit," as Dave Irwin's article in the *Tucson Weekly* in 1998 was headlined. Rafael Payan compared the situation to the construction of the church of San Xavier del Bac, the jewel of a Spanish mission just south of Tucson, begun in 1783. As long as the project was still under construction, taxes never had to be paid to Spain. As a result, the second tower of San Xavier was never completed. With Kartchner, it was a similar situation. "As long as we were building, we could collect funds from State Parks revenues," he noted. To Payan, this turned out to be a very good thing. "Every time something failed, we could then try something else," he says. "Let's do it right! We knew there would always be a revenue stream."

That year, 1998, the legislature, as part of its periodic "sunset" reviews of the purpose and functioning of state agencies, examined Arizona State Parks. The Speaker of the House at the time, Jeff Groscost, was determined to pressure State Parks to do something about the seemingly endless Kartchner project. So the legislature approved House Bill 2510 that stated that unless Kartchner Caverns State Park was opened by June 30, 2000—eighteen months from then—the state would halt all funding for the entire agency. If the park was completed by that date, the agency funding would be guaranteed for five years. And the Speaker was determined to make State Parks sweat. The continuation bill for the agency remained stuck in his pocket for weeks.

Supporters of Kartchner were outraged. In an editorial, the *Arizona Republic* called the bill "a bewildering example of legislative short-sightedness." The newspaper argued, "There is no need to rush. It must be done right," without artificial deadlines. Still, the *Republic* conceded that Speaker Groscost had put Governor Jane Dee Hull "between a rock and a hard place." If she vetoed the bill, Arizona State Parks would be forced to shut down.

The bill was finally enacted without the governor's signature. In a letter to Secretary of State Betsey Bayless, Hull explained that she hadn't signed the bill because she didn't find it good public policy. Kartchner was a "delicate bit of God's handiwork," she wrote, and it would be a tragedy to squander it. "I have asked State Parks Director Ken Travous to extend an invitation to all legislators to visit Kartchner during the interim in order they might see first-hand the many challenges of developing this natural treasure," she wrote. "I believe these visits may lead to a reconsideration of whether an arbitrary deadline is truly in the long-term best interest of our parks system, this state, and its citizens." Nonetheless, House Bill 2510 became law.

The legislature need not have worried about the delays, however. The completion of the Rotunda and Throne rooms complex was getting closer every day now. One of the last steps involved the design and installation of a lighting system. Lighting was tricky: the cave had to be illuminated for visitors to see its various features—no one had ever seen the chambers entirely lit up at that point—but the lights themselves had to be concealed from view. At the same time, it was crucial that the lighting not raise the temperature unduly within the cave or promote the growth of algae, which tend to flourish around lights and could eventually result in the growth of moss and even ferns.

Frank Florentine was an unorthodox choice to design the lighting for Kartchner Caverns. He was the lighting designer at the Smithsonian National Air and Space Museum in Bethesda, Maryland, and had a degree in theater. Ken Travous had been impressed by a magazine article that Florentine had written. Florentine had worked extensively in the world of ballet—with Rudolf Nureyev and at the Wolf Trap Foundation for the Performing Arts outside of Washington, D.C., where he worked for three seasons. But he had absolutely no experience in creating lighting for a cave.

When he entered the Rotunda and Throne rooms complex in late 1997, the first thing Florentine did was to turn off all the lights. He heard a drop of water that echoed throughout the cave. "I saw that one drop could create a lot of noise," said Florentine. "I realized that, in the dark, a little light can create a lot of light."

That became the basis of Florentine's approach to lighting Kartchner—not to change what people saw but to capture the cave as it was. It was an approach that, in his view, was not minimalist, but realist. "I tried to give the effect of a spelunker's headlight," he said. There would be no colored lights—they didn't look pure and also brought up maintenance issues—but he tried to use just a little more red than daylight in his lighting to bring out the iron in Kartchner's formations.

At first, Florentine viewed the cave as a six-month job that he could do in his spare time. In reality, it took him almost seven years, starting in late 1997 and ending with the opening of the Big Room in 2003. During his first two years—the period in which he lit the Rotunda and Throne rooms complex—he would fly out to Arizona every other weekend. He would leave Washington on a Thursday night, arriving at Kartchner by noon on Friday, when the construction crews would be finishing work. Then he would work the remainder of the day on Friday and all day Saturday when construction wasn't going on and he could have the run of the place, turning lights on and off as he required. "You needed darkness to focus," said Florentine. "We couldn't interrupt construction work time for lighting, and we had to make it all dark. The cave was dark—you would set the lights and do it without interrupting work." Then, during the week when he was gone, crews would lay the wiring.

In many respects, Florentine found that lighting a cave wasn't significantly different from lighting a ballet or a theatrical production. "Basically, it is all a big stage," he said. "The idea is to amaze people and to focus their attention just like in a ballet. It is all about light and shadows." Still, it was muddy, and makeshift lights were strewn across poles; the remnants of ongoing construction work were everywhere, even when no one was around. The area to be lit was far broader than a theatrical stage and was different from place to place. He couldn't move a stalagmite or a cave drapery from one place to another like props or people on a stage; dancers, after all, could move into the light. "You almost had to go through the cave one lamp at a time," said Florentine. The biggest technical challenge, he said, was "to light a path without lighting."

A computerized system controlled with dimmers was eventually installed to allow lights to be turned on and off as tours trooped through, and trail lighting was separated from feature lighting. Rope lights were built into the low walls along the trails.

One of the easiest features to light turned out to be Kubla Khan, the redwood-colored, five-story column that is the dramatic highlight of the Rotunda and Throne rooms complex tour. It was so large that it became simply a question of what the designer wanted to emphasize. State Parks had considered projecting scenes—an Arizona sunrise, for example—onto Kubla Khan as if it was a giant video screen, but such ideas were eventually scrapped. Kubla Khan needed no enhancement; it could more than stand on its own. In front of the column, a small amphitheater was created (a fake rock was even placed along the trail to block the view at first so the towering column became even more dramatic when it first came into view) for a light show that would provide a climax to tours of the cave. Visitors would sit on benches, gazing upon Kubla Khan and listening to the piped-in choral strains of the four-minute-long "Adiemus" from the group of the same name's album *Songs of Sanctuary.* Travous chose the music—with its elements of "New Age," world music, and classical traditions—over the objections of some who simply wanted a moment of silent meditation and grandeur. Originally, Tufts and Tenen had been strongly opposed to any music; the cave didn't require any help, in their view. But then the discoverers accompanied groups of visitors on two early tours of the cave. On the first, there was no music, and at the tour's climactic moment, they saw people sitting and gabbing on the benches overlooking Kubla Khan. On the second tour, however, as soon as the music started, the visitors stopped talking. "The second tour was a much superior experience," said Tenen, and both he and Tufts became converts to the idea of music.

In fact, "Adiemus" had an appropriately sacred quality to it, and compared to some of the gimmicks at other caves—the strains of "Oh Shenandoah" at Luray Caverns, for example—it was the epitome of dignity and good taste. Florentine analyzed the music and then melded the lights to the tempo, lighting the back and the front and the front and the ceiling. Four minutes of music required seventy light cues. And in the end was darkness, the unvarnished darkness of Kartchner Caverns.

Finally, on Friday, November 5, 1999, twenty-five years almost to the day when Tufts and Tenen first glimpsed Xanadu, the Rotunda and Throne rooms complex—but not yet the Big Room, with its bat habitat—was opened to the public for the first time. The total cost of more than eleven years of work was $28 million.

Tufts would say that it was a blessing that he had never explored the cave back when he was a teenager and had first noticed the sinkhole that led to Kartchner. "If I had found it then," he said, "I would have done the logical thing and told a caving club about it, or the Forest Service, or the sheriff. Then the cave probably would have become public knowledge, access would have been difficult to control, and it might have been destroyed as a result." He attributed his seven-year delay in finding Kartchner from that initial visit to the "cave god" at work. In his view, "The cave god said, 'You're not ready to find this yet.'"

At 5 a.m. on the day of the opening ceremony, November 5, 1999, Tufts and Tenen, sleepy but excited, paused at a gas station convenience store just off the interstate in Benson to down a cup of coffee before the festivities. "We should see if there is any coverage in the paper," Tufts suggested. They picked up the *Arizona Daily Star*, the Tucson newspaper, to be greeted with a large photo of themselves, in hard hats and peering out of the sinkhole, on the front page under the banner headline "A Deep, Dark Secret."

That day there was the inevitable ribbon-cutting featuring Governor Hull, as well as a grand-opening ceremony for what was called the "Jewel of the Desert" celebration. A multi-tiered platform was erected near the Discovery Center, and the entertainment included a color guard from nearby Fort Huachuca, the Tucson Symphony Orchestra, a Native American medicine man, video footage, and an auction to benefit the Friends of Kartchner Caverns. There was even a song, called "Moment by Moment," sung by a narrator and boys' chorus and composed expressly for the event, with the lyrics: "Moment by moment, nature astounds us / Beauty surrounds us everywhere / The soul of the cavern will capture your heart." Invited guests dined on southwestern cuisine and drank wine from southern Arizona vineyards.

Frank Florentine, the lighting designer, was there, and before the ceremony, at the top of the entrance, he saw Gary Tenen emerging from underground. He was convinced that Tenen would complain that he had ruined his cave. Instead, Tenen informed him it was the most beautiful cave he had ever seen. "I never saw a cave done so well," the discoverer told him. "You really captured the spirit of it."

That day, though, as Tufts and Tenen wandered through the cave, marveling at the lighted features as if they were seeing it for the first time, they could sense that something was wrong. The cave just didn't feel as wet and humid as it had in the past. The discoverers had noticed this on visits earlier that year, and State Parks officials had tried to reassure them; but today, amidst all the hoopla, it bothered them more than ever. Could the cave, despite all the elaborate efforts at care and conservation, somehow be drying out? Was the cave god uneasy after all?

THE EARLY DAYS of Arizona's new Kartchner Caverns State Park were a great triumph. In part because of the policy of restricting visitors to just over five hundred a day—out of concern that the heat generated by large numbers of people trooping through the cave could affect its microclimate—reservations were sold out for almost an entire year even though only the Rotunda and Throne rooms complex was open. The telephone lines in tiny Benson were overwhelmed during the first week of the opening, with ten thousand phone calls flooding a system that could barely handle two thousand. Construction was underway at the Big Room. Favorable media coverage in the *New York Times,* the *Los Angeles Times,* and dozens of other papers around the globe created national and international "buzz." For fiscal year 2000—the first complete year the park was open—the new state park boasted 199,060 visitors.

But all was not as well as it seemed to be to the admiring visitors who marveled at the stalagmites and cave draperies, marched single file through the "imaginary passage" from the Rotunda Room to the Throne Room, and sat in worshipful awe before Kubla Khan. The relative dryness of the cave continued to disturb Tufts and Tenen. On the night of the grand opening, once the color guard and the Tucson Symphony Orchestra and the honored guests had gone home, the cave discoverers huddled with Arizona State Parks official Jay Ream in the manager's office and expressed their concerns.

In a memo to Ream, dated January 13, 2000, two months later, Tufts and Tenen wrote, "The cave is distinctly drier as determined by simple observational evidence noticed by cavers. Confirming this, evaporation rates appear to be up significantly in the Rotunda and Throne rooms and apparently in the Big Room also." Statistics bore them out. During the pre-development studies in 1991 and 1992, the temperature at the lower Throne Room's environmental monitoring station had fluctuated between sixty-seven and sixty-eight degrees Fahrenheit and the humidity measured over 99 percent. Now, the temperature had risen by

Epilogue

four and a half degrees Fahrenheit, and the humidity had decreased by more than two percentage points. While to the layperson those numbers might seem a small difference, to those who studied caves, they represented a significant, even alarming, trend.

Despite the strenuous efforts made to preserve the cave's air flows and microclimate, something was awry. The changes in temperature and humidity started to occur during the period after construction started on the tunnels. Could it have been that energy from people, lights, and/or concrete curing had been responsible? Could water have been lost by evaporation through tunnels and doors? Could the decision not to mist the tunnels during the construction period (later reversed) have been a factor—or the fact that the tunnels were so large in themselves? On the other hand, in the mid-to-late 1990s, the years in which the cave started to dry out, southern Arizona began to experience a severe drought. Other nearby caves, like Colossal Cave outside Tucson, and wild caves in the Whetstone and nearby Huachuca mountains, appeared to be experiencing the same problems. Did the changes at Kartchner have more to do with the vagaries of the weather outside (and perhaps global climate change) than with any mistakes or carelessness during development? Or was some combination of man-made and natural factors the most likely explanation?

Tufts and Tenen were agitated, extremely so. If the drying and evaporation continued, the cave speleothems—the stalactites and stalagmites and other magnificent features, some of them more than 100,000 years

One of the exhibits inside the park's Discovery Center (Noelle Wilson, Arizona State Parks)

old—might be threatened. The wet, "living" cave that was Kartchner could eventually become a dry and dead one like Colossal. The two discoverers became increasingly frustrated with what they perceived as State Parks lethargy, if not denial, in confronting the issue. Arizona State Parks had put so much of its heart and soul into the cave, the discoverers believed, that agency officials simply wouldn't accept the idea that there might be problems. In their memo of January 13, 2000, Tufts and Tenen complained that even though there was a procedure in place for gathering data, there was no procedure for interpreting the data or what to do if the data indicated that something was wrong.

As it was, State Parks was feeling somewhat embattled. "After the opening of Throne/Rotunda, Gary and Randy read me the riot act about the drying of the cave," said Ream, who had been promoted in June 1998 to be the agency's chief of operations. "This happens on the day we opened Throne/Rotunda, and it's mine to deal with. Meanwhile, we've got pollution and *E. coli* at Slide Rock and *E. coli* at Lake Havasu [two other state parks]. There is low humidity and high temperature at

Kartchner. I've got Gary and Randy saying that State Parks is ruining that cave, that people are ruining that cave!" Ream was facing so many problems that he wondered if his promotion had been worth it.

In the midst of all this, as Ream noted, the irony was that Kartchner was sold out for a solid year, even though only part of the cave was open.

Later that year, on September 5, 2000, the *New York Times* published a lengthy, 2,116-word article that shined a national spotlight on Kartchner, calling attention to the problems at the cave. The article, written by Sandra Blakeslee, began this way:

> Take a sopping wet underground cavern in a remote corner of Arizona. Add a man-made entrance with heavy steel doors to keep out the hot desert air, a misting system to keep the cavern damp and lights to show off a wonderland of spires, flowstone, soda straws and other phantasmagorical cave formations.
>
> Then add a human being who, in a one-hour visit, sloughs off some 60,000 skin fragments, 160 million dust particles, 20,000 clothing-lint particles, 25 quarts of carbon dioxide gas and 170 watts of body heat. Multiply that by 183,000 visitors to the cave each year.

The upshot, the author wrote, was an "ad hoc experiment" to determine "if it is possible to bring thousands of people into the fragile environment of a pristine cave without destroying the cave in the process." The article cast doubt on that very possibility. It included a number of criticisms by cave experts, as well as comments from Randy Tufts. "Our main concern is that they [State Parks] don't seem to be on top of data collection," Tufts told the *Times*. "It's one thing to have a problem and know it and another to have a problem and not know it." Quotes from Executive Director Ken Travous in defense of State Parks were largely relegated to the latter part of the article, and State Parks agency staffers couldn't have been happy to have their new pride and joy described as "an ad hoc experiment."

Twelve days later, on September 17, the *Arizona Republic* published an op-ed piece by Tufts and Tenen in which they restated many of the same concerns, even more sharply. Although praising the "sincere commitment of Arizona State Parks," the cave discoverers charged that there had been little scientific inquiry since the initial baseline studies were finished in 1992. State Parks had continued to gather data, all right, but hadn't analyzed it. No one with knowledge of caves outside of Kartchner had been brought in; only within the previous three weeks (in anticipation of the *Times* article) had State Parks even approached a cave scientist, they contended. "To fix the immediate problems, cave experts should be summoned posthaste," the discoverers wrote. In addition, they suggested the hiring of a qualified cave science officer at Kartchner, with "real authority and influence," possibly reporting directly to the State Parks Board. They did conclude their piece somewhat hopefully: "Kartchner Caverns will not have to close. There should still be time to fix any problem if new studies verify that the changes do indeed threaten the cave."

Out of the public criticism emerged one positive result: State Parks hired its first full-fledged cave scientist, Rick Toomey, who became cave resource manager in April 2001. During his first year, Toomey installed some fifty data loggers to monitor temperature and humidity in the cave and tunnels and conducted daily, ongoing analysis of the findings. That obviously didn't stop the worrisome drying trends, both below- and aboveground. However, Toomey's appointment reassured Tufts and Tenen and the caving community, at least for the moment. Now, Kartchner had its own scientist to monitor data and to keep on top of the situation.

Changes in temperature and humidity weren't the only challenges facing the cave during its first years of operation. The nearby city of Benson had high expectations for the new state park—perhaps too high. Early estimates from local officials were that Kartchner might attract some 250,000 to 350,000 visitors a year. "If Carlsbad can do 600,000 people a year, why can't we?" demanded Benson's community development director, Larry Kreps. "There are a lot of people out there who think this will be bigger than State Parks ever said or guesstimated." The Cochise College Center for Economic Research estimated that, given the tourism "multiplier effect," the direct and indirect economic benefit of Kartchner to the Benson area could be within $19.5 million and $27.4 million for the park's initial operating year. In part because of anticipation of an economic bonanza, by 2000 the population of Benson jumped 23.2 percent from 1990, according to the U.S. Census Bureau, with most of the growth occurring since 1995. The sleepy town of 4,000 that had grown up around the Butterfield Stage and the Southern Pacific Railroad appeared ready for take-off.

But it didn't turn out quite the way Benson businessmen and city officials had hoped. For one thing, those estimates of 250,000 or 350,000 or 600,000 visitors didn't come true; State Parks was determined to limit the number of visitors—the agency saw this as an essential part of its stewardship of the cave—and the locals were unable to persuade it to change its position. In addition, many visitors bypassed Benson for lodging and meals—including Tufts and Tenen's picturesque hangout, the Horseshoe Café—opting to stay in Tucson or in neighboring Sierra Vista or Bisbee instead. Still, the town was benefiting to some degree: in 2000, Benson restaurant and bar sales were up 10.8 percent over the year before, unemployment was down, and an estimated 305 workers were directly employed as a result of economic activity relating to Kartchner Caverns.

So it wasn't surprising that when developer Helmut Horn of the Coastal Hotel Group proposed to build a resort on 180 acres on the north side of Kartchner, about a half mile from the cave, Benson was prepared to embrace it. Called Whetstone Springs, the $40 million resort would include 216 luxury villas and 128 casitas, to say nothing of a spa, a lodge, an amphitheater, a grocery store, a restaurant, swimming pools, tennis courts, and even a helicopter pad. (The designer of the resort was a Scottsdale firm called Taliesin Architects, successor firm to the practice of architect Frank Lloyd Wright; Horn himself was an amateur photographer whose work would be later be shown in a Tucson gallery.) Estimates were that Whetstone Springs would bring a welcome $500,000 in tax revenues yearly to the city's coffers. In early July 2001, Benson's Planning and Zoning Commission approved the rezoning of the property by a five-to-one vote. The developers emphasized that they would avoid any damage to the cave by pumping water from wells two to three miles downstream from Kartchner and treating wastewater on site.

The proposal was scheduled to go before the Benson City Council in early September, and it caused an outcry. The area proposed for development shared the same limestone block as the cave itself, prompting widespread fears that contaminated water from the spa or the resort's other attractions could travel through underground fissures and pollute the cave. State Parks Executive Director Ken Travous called the resort "a really bad idea," and the agency offered developer Horn $1 million for the property (he had paid $800,000); he declined the offer. The Phoenix and Tucson newspapers editorialized against it ("Don't Cave In," headlined an editorial in the *Arizona Daily Star).* "If some yahoo at the resort decided to dump a 55-gallon drum of cleaner or solvent, we don't know where it will go at this point," said Don Young, consulting hydrologist at the park. And in a report completed for State Parks, nationally known hydrogeologist Tom Aley stated, "Aside from wishful thinking, there are no credible hydrologic or geologic data to indicate that the proposed development would not degrade Kartchner Caverns . . ." Aley himself had performed an experiment to test the possibility of contamination, placing fluorescent dye in a wash at the proposed resort site, then immediately driving over to the cave and discovering that indeed there were signs of the dye at Kartchner.

Meanwhile, some questioned whether the developers were really serious about building a resort in the first place, if the entire proposal wasn't just a ploy to raise the value of the land and make a tidy profit for those involved with it.

On September 3, 2001, the Benson City Council held a public hearing before an overflow crowd of seventy-five. Developer Horn insisted that his twelve other hotels were "anchored around an environmental belief . . . We have a flawless track record." Jean Emery, who headed up resource management for State Parks, told the council that people "can't control" the cave. "But there is one thing that we have complete control of," she said. "We can wreck it." In attendance, as well, was Randy Tufts. "We need to look way ahead," Tufts told the councilors. "We're not just talking about something that will have a thirty-year lifetime." A 3,800-gallon diesel spill near Mammoth Cave in Kentucky just a week before gave opponents more ammunition; the Mammoth spill could have released chemicals into a spring that connects to the caves there. After three hours of public discussion, the council decided to put off a vote.

In the end, it didn't matter what the Benson City Council decided. A few months later, in January 2002, Arizona State Parks went to court to begin the process of acquiring 160 of the 180 acres proposed for the resort by eminent domain. On April 13, 2004, the agency paid $1.624 million for the property. It was only the second time in the State Parks agency's 44-year history that it had acquired land in a "hostile takeover." Kartchner had been saved from potential contamination, but the whole affair proved a windfall for the developers: they wound up with double the $800,000 they had originally paid for the property.

At the Benson public hearing, Randy Tufts had said, "When Gary and I crawled into that cave . . . We never thought we'd come out in a City Council chamber. My faith has always been that if you get people talking to each other, everything will work out." At the meeting, Tufts spoke through a surgical mask; he was on immunosuppressive drugs and needed to avoid infection. It would be his last public appearance.

———————————

In 1990, at the age of forty-two, Randy Tufts had gone back to school, at the University of Arizona, as a graduate student in the geosciences. Tufts had been interested in space exploration since his boyhood, and for a number of years now, a subject that increasingly intrigued him was Europa, one of the four moons of the planet Jupiter. He began to devour literature articles about Europa, discovered by Galileo in 1610, whose size is about the same as earth's moon. What really excited him was the possibility of life on Europa, something that also had excited his hero, Carl Sagan, who Tufts had buttonholed in an Ithaca, New York, parking lot thirteen years before. The Voyager spacecraft had made two flybys of Jupiter in 1979, coming within one hundred thousand miles of Europa. The low-resolution photos it had sent back, crude as they were, were fascinating to a geologist and cave explorer: images of strange, scalloped ridges that snaked across Europa's icy surface in a pattern whose significance no one could quite figure out.

It was in 1993 or so that the forty-something graduate student showed up in the UA's Lunar and Planetary Laboratory at the office of Dr. Richard Greenberg. "I want to study Europa," Tufts announced, knowing that it was one of Greenberg's special interests too. Greenberg remembered his arrival as "kind of out of the blue." The professor of planetary sciences vaguely knew who Tufts was and thought he "seemed like a smart guy." But no one at the university was really working on Europa at that point, so all Greenberg could do was to encourage Tufts to continue his course work and keep in touch.

Two years later, all this had changed. The National Aeronautics and Space Administration's (NASA) Galileo probe, launched in 1989, was orbiting Jupiter and its moons, and Greenberg was a member of Galileo's imaging team, working closely with NASA. Tufts returned to the Lunar and Planetary Laboratory, joined Greenberg's research group, and Greenberg took him on as a grad student, becoming co-advisor on Tufts's thesis.

For Randy Tufts, it was the beginning of a brilliant second career. The imaging team was an integrated group in which everyone had his or her specialty: Tufts was the classical geologist of the team. At this point, Galileo began to send back startling photographs of Europa, far more precise than those Voyager had sent back more than fifteen years before. (Galileo came within 124 miles of the moon, in contrast to Voyager which passed by at a distance of one hundred thousand miles.) Soon after, in 1996, the discoverer of Kartchner Caverns made another geologic discovery, perhaps even more significant than that of the cave—a twisting 810-kilometer fault line on the surface of Europa that was the length of California's San Andreas Fault and was later called the Astypalaea Linea. "Randy would always say 'The Cave' when referring to Kartchner," noted Greenberg. "Now, he would always say, 'The Fault,' in reference to the long fault that he had discovered. It was amazingly parallel."

But Tufts's discovery went beyond just discovering a fault on the moon of another planet. Working with other members of the team,

Tufts plotted a model that indicated that the fault couldn't possibly have developed unless there was, or had been, a large body of water under the surface. Jupiter's massive size—three hundred times that of earth—would result in tides on Europa's ocean, causing it to rise one hundred feet (compared to earth's tides of four to six feet) and thus forcing the thin icy surface crust to crack, creating the fault and other ridge-like surface features. The fault couldn't exist on an ice surface like that of Europa if there was merely solid rock below.

It was the likelihood of a liquid ocean under the surface of Europa that indicated to scientists that there might be life there. Assuming that the icy crust was less than ten kilometers thick, as Greenberg surmised, it might crack under pressure from Jupiter's tides and allow water from Europa's subsurface ocean to well up in the cracks, absorbing the sun's energy and thus allowing life to develop. This possibility caused great interest and debate among planetary scientists, who advocated strongly for a new orbiter that would further investigate Europa's ocean. (NASA scrapped the idea in 2002, however, due to budget cuts.)

And it particularly intrigued Tufts. As he told *The New Yorker* magazine writer Michael Benson, "It always seemed to me that if we found life someplace else it would give us a vastly new perspective on existence. And we would probably realize that we weren't quite as important as we thought we were. I mean, it might take us down a peg, which could always be useful." (Tufts put it similarly in his Ph.D. dissertation: " . . . when we humans find extraterrestrial life, wherever it is, its discovery will have a deep, positive effect on our thinking. The meaning of that discovery may be this: that Life is what the Universe 'does,' and is to be treasured all the more. If such a realization is the result, what more practical benefit can this search have?")

In December, 1998, at age fifty, Tufts received his Ph.D. in the department of geosciences. His dissertation was entitled "Lithospheric Displacement Features on Europa and their Interpretation."

Tufts's discovery in outer space provided an uncanny parallel to his discovery under the earth in the limestone hills of southern Arizona. Echoing his own apprehensions at Kartchner, he became increasing concerned that if life did exist on Europa, future space probes might possibly contaminate it. To Greenberg, the similarities between Tufts's work on Kartchner and on Europa were not just what Tufts discovered but also how he approached things. "Randy had obsessive goals," he said. "In high school, he wanted to find a cave. Everything was directed toward this. He went to college, got a degree in geology in order to achieve that goal. The same approach can be seen in Europa. He had the same directed, deliberate, obsessive goal." And the political skills that Tufts had refined in college and in his efforts to get the cave developed also served him well on the Europa project. "Randy knew how to work the politics of the space mission," said Greenberg. "I'd often send him to meetings within Galileo where he would be more effective than I was."

In May 2000, Greenberg and Tufts made a trip to the Arctic Ocean at Barrow, Alaska, under the auspices of the Discovery Channel, which was making a TV show about the moons of the solar system. The two researchers were eager to see if the Arctic might provide any analogs to what they were seeing on Europa. Greenberg noticed that Tufts was having trouble handling a snowmobile—on one occasion, Tufts rolled the machine onto Greenberg's leg—but ascribed it to his being "a kid from the desert." A few weeks later, back in Tucson, Tufts began to complain of back pains. He went to see a doctor and was diagnosed with a rare and potentially fatal blood disease called myeleodyplastic syndrome (MDS). It was the same disease that had killed the astronomer Carl Sagan a few years before.

Gary Tenen reveled in family life. He took his children caving and hiking and cooked Shabbat dinner every Friday evening for Judy and the kids (even baking his own challah bread); as the children got older, family dinners became colloquia on the great issues of the day. For the unmarried Randy Tufts, the Tenens were, in many respects, his family: he would take young David and Julia and Levi up on their parents' roof and show them the stars and planets through a telescope. Then, in 1997, while working on his doctorate at the University of Arizona, he met Ericha Scott, an art therapist with a specialty in the treatment of trauma, who had recently moved to Tucson from Dallas. She was working on her internship through the UA.

They met at the Siddha Yoga Center, which focused on chanting as a way of meditation. Ericha, who had long been interested in Eastern spiritual practice, had gone there "to chant the names of God," as she put it. Randy, who was in the middle of working on his dissertation, was there to help relieve stress; a friend had suggested that chanting might relax him. The first time Ericha saw him was when Randy was asked to clean the women's restroom. "There he was with a scrub brush in one hand and Comet in the other and talking really fast and his hands were moving," recalled Ericha. "And I thought, 'This guy is a little bit different.' I was sort of tickled by it." Still, it was another four or five months before they really took notice of one another. That was followed by months of spending time together after yoga, just talking—about life, religious ideas, science, Europa, about Ericha's dissertation. After one discussion about the French philosopher Descartes and the mind/

body split, according to Ericha's account, Randy left the conversation thinking "She is not as much of a flake as I thought!" And Ericha left the conversation convinced "He's not such a nerd after all!"

They knew things were getting serious when they brought their respective dissertations to show each other at a Siddha Yoga breakfast. Both manuscripts were three hundred pages, and Randy brought his in a box—it hadn't been bound yet. It was flirting, graduate student–style. Both their dissertations were fairly arcane. Ericha's was on dissociative-disordered women who self-mutilate, while Randy's was on the Jovian moon Europa and the fault that he had discovered there.

What impressed Ericha was the scope of Randy's knowledge. "He could talk about anything," she said. "He was truly a Renaissance man, as much as anyone I've known. It is hard to grasp the depth and breadth of his intellect. The areas of knowledge and wisdom he had were so amazing. And it was so integrated."

Soon their after-yoga conversations evolved into dating, and a year and a half after they met, they moved in together. Randy had just turned fifty; Ericha was in her early forties. He graduated in 1998; she received her Ph.D. in March of 1999 and was hired shortly after for a part-time faculty position at Prescott College. (She soon was running the counseling psychology program there, building it up from five students to twenty-five.) "I really liked how our relationship developed," Ericha said. "There was an innocence to it and a sweetness that was very touching. The more I got to know Randy, the more handsome and precious I found him to be."

Even when they were first going out, Randy didn't talk much about Kartchner Caverns, which hadn't opened to the public yet. He mentioned that he had discovered a cave, but Ericha didn't pay it too much heed: she thought about the caves she had crawled around in West Texas when she was a kid that were hardly caves at all. It wasn't until a year and a half after she first met him that he took her to the cave. "It was important to him that I liked him for just who he was, and that I didn't know about the cave," she said.

By the time Kartchner was poised to open to the public in November 1999, Randy was "living, breathing, sleeping" the cave once again. At the grand opening—the couple was living together by then—Ericha recalls strangers coming up to him with tears in their eyes; they were so moved by what they had seen. When she asked Randy what it was going to be like for him when he went back to work and all the hoopla died down, he told her, "No problem." About Thursday of the following week he came home and complained, "No one wants to talk about it anymore!" Later, he admitted wandering through a local mall hoping someone would recognize him, but passed it off as a joke. (He kept the

Randy Tufts and Ericha
Scott Tufts (Barry Zak)

subject alive though, giving seventy-five talks and lectures about the cave during the year after it opened.)

In the summer of 2000, after the couple had had been together less than two years, Randy was diagnosed with myeleodyplastic syndrome. He opted to have a bone marrow transplant. Even then, his chances of survival were only 50 to 70 percent. His only sibling, younger sister Judy Rodin, a Tucson nurse, volunteered to serve as the donor and was discovered to be a "match." The transplant had to happen fast, within a few months. Things were further complicated by the fact that Ericha herself had been diagnosed with breast cancer seven months before; she cured herself through alternative therapies and wasn't given a clean bill of health till a week after his diagnosis.

Three days before the transplant, on October 22, 2000, Randy and Ericha were married at the Southside Presbyterian Church in Tucson. Southside was a church whose interest in social and political issues appealed to the couple. The church had been the first location in the United States to declare itself a sanctuary for refugees from the Central American civil wars in the 1980s, and John Fife, the minister who married them, was a legendary figure in Tucson, having served six months in jail while awaiting trial for his role in the Sanctuary Movement. It was a complicated, tumultuous period for Randy and Ericha, planning a transplant procedure and a wedding at the same time.

Randy had already lost twenty pounds and all his hair, from pre-transplant chemotherapy drugs. He hadn't talked about his illness publicly at that point, and many of those in attendance weren't aware of it. The invitation, sent just a few days before, urged the guests to donate money to the Randy Tufts Transplant Fund, in lieu of wedding gifts. Two hundred and twenty people showed up to the wedding; outside, it was pouring rain. Randy and Ericha decided they would take some time during the service to explain Randy's condition and what he was soon to undergo. They did so. But there were moments of levity, too. During the service, Randy asked Ericha to introduce herself to those who didn't know her, and she said she was from Texas. Then Randy added, "Many of you know that I'm a native, unlike Ericha, but more and more I'm feeling like a transplant." The entire crowd at the church groaned. Randy was famous for his bad puns.

The transplant appeared to be a success. In many respects, it was like a simple blood transfusion. Ericha, Gary Tenen, and others close to him were there for the procedure. "It was a kind of ceremony," Randy later said. He remained in the hospital for three weeks, while his sister's bone marrow took root in his body and his immune system reconstituted itself. The risk for infection was high. With his blood cell counts rising, he went home, although he remained vulnerable to infection and to rejection of the bone marrow. "Here I am, 52, and still afraid of rejection," he quipped.

For the next year or so Randy seemed to be doing relatively well, and he was hoping to return to work at the Lunar and Planetary Laboratory. He was determined to be very public about his bone marrow transplant and the importance of a bone marrow donor registry. The Tucson papers covered his transplant and recovery extensively. (This gave him the opportunity for some more bad jokes: "I experience side-effects, therefore I am," he said, echoing Descartes.) Randy was named the honorary chair and patient ambassador for the Tucson Light the Night Walk to raise funds for the Leukemia and Lymphoma Society. His activism on the subject led him to become an advocate for Carlos Valencia, a Tucson teenager suffering from leukemia who became a local cause celebre as a result of a series of drives to find a bone marrow match for the teen. In the aftermath of the publicity surrounding Carlos's story—and Randy's—the bone marrow registry in Tucson grew by six thousand. (Carlos died in 2004 at age 16.)

It was almost a year after the transplant that Randy, wearing his surgical mask to avoid infection, attended the Benson public meeting regarding the proposed spa development near Kartchner. Randy was strongly opposed to the proposal, and Ericha went with him to the meeting. "It was a very elegant presentation," she recalled. "Everyone was riveted. A TV station interviewed him that night. They paid attention to what he had to say."

The meeting took place in September, but by December, he began a downhill slide. In March, he was back in the hospital, this time in intensive care. That first night, forty people came in to hear Ericha report on Randy's condition over dinner in the hospital cafeteria. Ericha moved into the intensive care ward, and each evening, she would come down to the cafeteria to give friends an update. After eighteen days in the intensive ward, Bruce Randall Tufts died on April 1, 2002—April Fools' Day—at the age of 53. Ericha, who had been at his side throughout, was there when he died. Also present were Gary Tenen and his children, David, Julia, and Levi; Randy's mother Carol; and his sister Judy.

"This is an adventure," Randy had told Ericha during the period after his transplant when it looked like he might make it. "This is interesting. This is way too interesting to miss. I wouldn't miss it for the world."

––––––––––––––––––––

It was all a great adventure—from the discovery of the cave, the beauty and mystery of it all, the years of "Lewis and Clark," the politicking, the development, the grand opening, and then, for Randy, the tragedy of a bizarre and fatal disease. With Randy's death, Gary Tenen was the last man standing. He became the steward of Kartchner Caverns, a role that he had played in the past but often in the shadow of Randy. Randy had represented the public face of the cave, the vision behind it, the political genius of its unfolding. Gary's role had been a critical complement; he was, as Randy's wife Ericha put it, "the strategist," "a rock," sometimes even "a bulldozer." Now, he was alone. He was the one asked to speak at schools and organizations, who, from outside, had to fight the bureaucratic battles over issues like the increasing dryness of the cave, still a serious concern even after the hiring of a cave scientist.

In 2003, the Big Room opened, behind schedule as the Rotunda and Throne rooms complex had been, but also a great success. Randy Tufts was not alive to witness it. Much of what had been learned from the work on the other chamber was put to good use here. During the Big Room construction period, work had ceased from the end of April to early September (and so did visitation once the Big Room opened); the bats remained protected and continued to return to the cave every spring to roost. For visitors, the Big Room was a longer tour than that of the upper cave, less spectacular perhaps, but more intimate, closer to the formations.

The conservation ethic that U.S. cavers had initiated in the 1960s and '70s, which Tufts and Tenen had continued in their years as stewards of Kartchner, and which had become so much the approach of Ken Travous and others in developing and managing the cave, was the hallmark of the new Kartchner Caverns State Park. Tufts and Tenen had "taken nothing but pictures, left nothing but footprints" (the latter on the muddy floor of the Rotunda Room pointed out to tour groups), as the National Speleogical Society motto went; the Kartchner family had done the same. During development, a supreme effort was made to protect the cave, even if it was not always entirely successful, and even if it led to delays and more difficult working conditions. Once the cave opened, the number of tourists was limited, visitors would stand in line dutifully to have their clothes misted, and guides would patiently explain that the features were growing so they couldn't be touched, that everyone had to stay on the trail. And no one was allowed into the Big Room for a substantial part of the year to protect the bat habitat, a stern conservation lesson in itself.

Everyone involved with the cave treated it with reverence. In the Discovery Center, visitors stared in awe at a display of Randy Tufts's heavy boots and black and red worn backpack, and Gary Tenen's cave helmet. As a thirteen-year-old, Levi Tenen noticed three kinds of reactions from visitors when he accompanied his father on visits to Kartchner: there were the people who came up to shake his father's hand, there were others who would follow him around and just stare, and then there were people who would keep looking and looking and finally summon the courage to talk to him. Everyone who had worked on the cave at almost any point seemed to have taken it to their hearts. Volunteers would come for the winter, living in trailers on the campground. "Randy and Gary had such love for it," said Rafael Payan, one of the State Parks development triumvirate. "Their philosophy seemed to extend to everyone involved." Larry Hawke, one of the legislators responsible for the acquisition of "Secret Cave," noted that during his tenure in the Arizona legislature, members didn't really make much money and lasting achievements were few. "But here was something you could really point to and be proud of being involved with," he observed. "It's there. There is so much you can't really point to. But this was good. You done good." To Dean Kartchner, the cave had given him "more experiences than I would have ever had otherwise." To Ken Travous, his involvement with the cave was a year-round "birthday present"; whenever he showed up at Kartchner, he felt like "Elvis in Disneyland."

In Travous's view, Tufts and Tenen had set the stage for the whole operation with a sense of stewardship and a conservation ethic that had been transmitted to those who came after them. "They set the bar high,

Randy Tufts and Gary Tenen in front of mesquite trees at the cave site (Gary Tenen)

and we set it two feet higher, and the people who came after us have set it two feet higher," said Travous. "They know the cave is there for the public, and at the same time, they know it is a continuing process forever that has to go on. Our conservation ethic in this country is a lot better than it was thirty years ago. I don't know if thirty years ago we could have pulled off what we pulled off at Kartchner Caverns."

The cave continues to be a huge success for Arizona State Parks, a "cash cow" even, with user fees far outpacing those of any of the other parks in the system. In fiscal 2003, the year the Big Room opened, there were 186,816 visitors; in fiscal 2004, there were 203,378; in fiscal 2005, there were 198,374. (In the fiscal year 2006, the number of visitors declined to 160,467, in part due to high gas prices, in the view of State Parks officials.) The total cost to develop the park, buildings, cave, and infrastructure was $34.6 million, only 10 percent of which had come from general revenue funds. Kartchner remains a national and international model for cave development, studied by scientists and cave specialists.

The cave was beautiful, the story of its discovery and protection was inspiring, but what would happen in thirty or fifty or one hundred years? So many of the officials involved in the purchase and construction of the park remained at Arizona State Parks in the years since Kartchner opened. The cave had been the making of careers. What would happen once they eventually departed, and individuals who didn't have their passion and proprietary attitude toward the cave took their places? More worrisome, would the cave continue to dry out, especially as human beings degraded the environment aboveground, and global warming threatened the Southwest with parching, perpetual heat, and drought? The slow drying-out of Kartchner remains a source of great concern, with no real solutions in sight, something that continues to preoccupy Gary Tenen.

The cave god, as Randy Tufts always called him (or her), had taken a supreme risk in permitting two young Arizona spelunkers to enter a cave so jealously guarded and cut off from the rest of the world for 200,000 years or more. The two men had not betrayed the cave god's trust, nor had their successors at State Parks. As Tufts noted, when the Iroquois Nation made decisions, tribal elders would always ask, "What effect will this have on the seventh generation to come?" The discoverers and, later, State Parks officials had tried to keep this in mind. But an infinitesimal moment in the history of a small cave in the Whetstone Mountains—the moment when Tufts and Tenen crawled into the blowhole and, man, with all his imperfections, entered the picture—might, in the end, prove as decisive as the tectonic shifts, the tumbling limestone, and the seeping water of geologic eons past.

Still, there was hope; there had to be. As Tufts wrote in one of his journals, speaking of caves, and relationships too: "Look at Kubla Khan. Drop by drop, moment by moment. Life, a relationship. The form evolves—always beautiful, always unexpected. Never predictable. It may go through periods of drought and periods of moisture, and may take years or millennia . . . Inexorable, persistent, beautiful in its imperfection and only given meaning through the eyes of a beholder. The cave is not there because the rock is intact, but because it is broken. The formation is not there because the drop was secure, but because it fell. It has beauty not because we are one with it but because we are separated, standing back to see. The hill is plain but contains in its heart, elegance and grace."

ACKNOWLEDG-MENTS

A number of people were extremely instrumental in the creation of this book. I am particularly grateful to Gary Tenen for his confidence in me and for the many generous and patient hours he spent in conversation over a three-year period, as well as our caving trips to Cave of the Bells and through the original route into Kartchner. Without the many doors that Gary opened, I could never have written this book. I can't thank him enough. Thanks to the entire Tenen family—Gary, Judy, David, Julia, and Levi—for their friendship, warmth, and hospitality. I'm also grateful to Carol Tufts, Ericha Scott Tufts, and Judy Tufts Rodin for sharing their recollections and perspectives about Randy's life and the cave. I am deeply appreciative of their trust in me and their many kindnesses. Thanks to members of the Kartchner family, in particular Dean, Mark, Max, and Kathy Kartchner, for their help in understanding the family's role in the history of the cave. Jay Ziemann at Arizona State Parks was crucial in explaining many important aspects of the Kartchner acquisition and development phase. Ginger Nolan was a superb guide to portions of Kartchner that visitors don't usually see and was full of information about the development of the cave. Larry Hawke guided me through the intricacies of the legislative process. I'm especially grateful to Dan Campbell for filling me in on The Nature Conservancy's role in the cave's acquisition and for sharing many recollections and details. Jay Ziemann and Steve Holland read the manuscript in its entirety and were generous with their time and advice. Thanks also to the Arizona Historical Society in Tucson, especially Leslie Broughton, for being so helpful during the many hours I spent looking through the Randy Tufts Collection. My gratitude also goes to the Friends of Kartchner Caverns for their generous support of this book.

I would also like to thank: Arizona State Parks, Ellen Bilbrey, Dolores Brouillette, Bob and Debbie Buecher, Marshall Colley, Michael Downing, David Gilbert and David Farnath, Rick Greenberg, Karen and Lyle Hymer-Thompson, Stephen McCauley, Leon Miller, Bill Peachey, Bill

Roe, Stephanie, Kate, and Bill Sklar, Steve Stokowski, Jonathan Strong, Ken Travous, and Harry Walker.

At Zachary Shuster Harmsworth, I am indebted to my agent Todd Shuster for his enthusiasm and assistance and also to Sandra Shagat and Joel Pulliam. At the University of Arizona Press, thanks especially to my redoubtable editor Patti Hartmann, to Christine Szuter, and to Nancy Arora and Sharon Hunt. Above all, I express my gratitude to my partner Paul Brouillette for encouraging me to take on this project, for being so loving and supportive during the writing of it, and for being such a thoughtful and clear-eyed reader.

200,000 BCE (and before) The cave today known as Kartchner
 Caverns forms in the Whetstone Mountains of southern Arizona.

192,000 BCE Date of earliest known formation in cave.

Summer 1967 Randy Tufts and companions lower themselves into the
 sinkhole but do not enter cave.

November 1974 Randy Tufts and Gary Tenen crawl into the blowhole
 and discover the cave they call Xanadu.

February 20, 1978 Tufts and Tenen visit James A. Kartchner and tell
 him of a cave on his land.

May 6, 1978 Mr. Kartchner and sons visit the cave for the first time.

December 1984 Tufts approaches Arizona State Parks about the
 possibility of acquiring and developing the cave.

April 14, 1985 Arizona governor Bruce Babbitt visits the cave.

Spring 1987 Kenneth E. Travous becomes director of Arizona State
 Parks.

February 1988 Kartchner family agrees to terms proposed by The
 Nature Conservancy for purchase of the cave and surrounding
 property by Arizona State Parks.

April 4, 1988 Arizona Senate finds Governor Evan Mecham guilty of
 two counts of "high crimes and misdemeanors."

April 27, 1988 Arizona legislature approves Bill 1188, acquiring the
 cave and surrounding property as James and Lois Kartchner State
 Park. Governor Rose Mofford signs the bill into law.

August 1995 Tunneling begins at Kartchner Caverns.

April 1997 Miners break through from the tunnels to the cave proper,
 and trail construction work begins in earnest.

November 5, 1999 Rotunda and Throne rooms complex is open to the
 public for the first time.

April 1, 2002 Cave discoverer Randy Tufts dies at age 53.

November 2003 Big Room opens for public tours.

PEOPLE INTERVIEWED

Bruce Babbitt

Brad Barber

Cindy Bethard

Ron Bridgemon

Bob Buecher

Debbie Buecher

Dan Campbell

Scott Davis

Jeff Dexter

Charles Eatherly

Dick Ferdon

Frank Florentine

Rick Greenberg

Larry Hawke

Steve Holland

Dean Kartchner

Kathy Kartchner

Mark Kartchner

Max Kartchner

John Kromko

Joe Lane

Ginger Nolan

Rafael Payan

Bill Peachey

Jay Ream

Judy Rodin

Bill Roe

David Tenen

Gary Tenen

Judy Tenen

Julia Tenen

Levi Tenen

Rick Toomey

Kenneth E. Travous

Carol Tufts

Ericha Scott Tufts

Jay Ziemann

NOTES

CHAPTER ONE: THE DISCOVERY

"An Overcast, Cool November Afternoon": Tufts, *History,* 12.

"Date unknown": Ibid, "List of Specifically Recollected or Recorded Trips, Rosters, Observations," 1.

Expedition to French Joe Canyon: Author interview with Gary Tenen, July 2006.

Tufts's teenage foray into Whetstones: Tufts, *History,* 10.

"There's a hell of a hole here": Ibid.

Tufts and Tenen discovery of the cave: Author interviews with Gary Tenen, April 2003, January 2004, and subsequent conversations. Also, Tufts, *History,* 13–15. Also, Negri, *Kartchner Caverns State Park,* 10–13.

CHAPTER TWO: TWO SPELUNKERS

Randy Tufts sneaks into Colossal Cave: Author conversation with Bill Peachey and Carol Tufts, January 2006.

Tufts childhood and family: Author interviews with Carol Tufts and Judy Rodin, May 2005 and January 2006.

Tenen background: Author interviews with Gary Tenen, June 2005 and January 2006.

Tufts and Tenen's caving methods and discovery of Red Cave: Tenen interview, April 2003.

"They had a scientific understanding of all this": Author interview with John Kromko, January 2006.

"Either you loved it or hated it": Tenen interview, April 2003.

Appeal of caving for Tenen: Author interview with Judy Tenen, June 2005.

University of Arizona in the 1960s and '70s: Author interviews with John Kromko, Gary Tenen, and Brad Barber.

"I just couldn't live with myself": Author interview with Carol Tufts, May 2005.

"No one had ever seen him in a sport coat and tie": Author interview with Brad Barber, May 2005.

"Randy had the ability to say one sentence": Ibid.

"He was very smooth, but not in a sleazy way": Ibid.

"The newest group of junior administrators, freshly scrubbed and beaming": Nihilist Organization poster, courtesy of Gary Tenen.

"The basic battle between them was over student control of student funds": Barber interview.

Merlin's bar: Ibid.

"I don't think that I ever before or since": Kromko interview.

Friends assumed he would go into politics: Ibid.

CHAPTER THREE: THE GOLDEN AGE OF ARIZONA CAVING

National Environmental Policy Act and Earth Day: Cahalan, *Edward Abbey: A Life,* 123.

"It was the golden age": Author interview with Bill Peachey, January 2005.

"In principle, caving is lot like climbing": Cahill, "The CO_2 Chronicles."

"Within seconds you lose sight of your starting point": Brucker and Watson, *The Longest Cave,* xvii.

"You were like foxhole buddies": Peachey interview.

Growth rates of speleothems: Moore and Sullivan, *Speleology,* 23.

"A lot of the destruction happened back in the 1940s": Author interview with Bob Buecher, June 2005.

Tufts and Tenen witness vandalism at Cave of the Bells: Author conversation with Gary Tenen, January 2004.

"Break, break-off, crack, carve, carve upon": Title 13, Article 14, *Arizona Revised Statutes,* Section 13-1025.

Onyx Cave gate problems: Brown, "Onyx Events Calendar."

"Who will win this never-ending battle?": Ibid.

"Best Wishes to all for 1975": Escabrosa Grotto balance statement, December 31, 1974.

"The time was right, the techniques were there": Peachey interview.

CHAPTER FOUR: EXPLORING XANADU

Tufts and Tenen's second visit to cave: Author interviews with Gary Tenen, April 2003, January 2004, and July 2006. Also, Tufts, *History,* 15–16.

"I thought we were dreaming": See video, "Jewel of the Desert," Kartchner Caverns State Park.

"In Xanadu did Kubla Khan": Coleridge, *The Portable Coleridge,* 157.

Tufts and Tenen drive to Xanadu: Tufts, *History,* 12. Also, author conversations with Gary Tenen, January 2004 and January 2006.

"Generally you didn't want a lot of food": Author interview with Gary Tenen, January 2006.

Horseshoe Café: Ibid.

Early explorations of Xanadu: Tufts, *History,* 15–20. Also, author interviews with Gary Tenen, January 2006 and July 2006.

Description of cave formation and geology: Moore and Sullivan, *Speleology,* 7–31, and Jackson, *Underground Worlds,* 68–69.

Brad Barber and bats: Author interview with Barber, May 2005.

"It was like walking through pancake batter or peanut butter": Tenen interview, April 2003.

Rattlesnakes in the sinkhole: Ibid.

Tenen in the pit: Ibid.

"A little annoyance": Ibid.

"In the center [of the Throne Room] sits a 55-foot column": Tufts letter to Harry Walker, undated, Randy Tufts Collection, Arizona Historical Society.

"Xanadu has the significance of an original Van Gogh": Tufts, *History,* 19.

"Holy and enchanted": Coleridge, *The Portable Coleridge,* 157.

CHAPTER FIVE: PLAYING FOR TIME

"Uranium traces around the Whetstone Mountains": Wilbur, "Uranium Rush Moves Closer to Tucson."

"The cave had not asked to be discovered": Tufts, *History,* 21.

Grotto meeting descriptions: Author interviews with Gary Tenen and also with Scott Davis, June 2006.

"In the beginning there were three or four of us, and we were super-secretive": Davis interview.

"The first question most people ask is 'Where are the caves?'": *An Introduction to the Escabrosa Grotto.*

"Always wear hiking boots and a Sierra Club T-shirt": Holland, "The Frustrated Caver's Guide to Finding Secret Caves in Arizona."

"There were a handful of caves in Arizona that everyone knew about": Author interview with Steve Holland, January 2004.

Peachey background: Randy Tufts interview with Bill Peachey, April 1989.

"I make caves disappear": Author interview with Bill Peachey, January 2005.

La Tetera Cave: Simonson, "'New' Cave Yields Deep Secrets." See also, Kimble, "Beyond Colossal."

"Essentially Randy had disappeared, Gary, too": Peachey interview.

"Controlled protection . . . that will provide protection for this natural resource": Gurnee, "Conservation through Commercialization."

Howe Caverns story: Folsom, *Exploring American Caves,* 99–103.

"Hitching per se has been very enjoyable": Randy Tufts letter to Gary Tenen and Brad Barber, August 20, 1977, Randy Tufts Collection, Arizona Historical Society.

"Our intent also is to make this a very educational cave": Randy Tufts letter to Harry Walker, undated, Tufts Collection.

"We spent ten times the hours planning and thinking" and "If it was left to Randy, we'd still be thinking about it": Author interview with Gary Tenen, January 2006.

CHAPTER SIX: ENCOUNTERING THE KARTCHNERS

Kartchner property: Author interview with Mark Kartchner, January 2004.

"You know, it sounds like these hills are hollow": Nero, *Kartchner Caverns State Park,* 6.

Tufts and Tenen trip to visit the Kartchners: Author interview with Gary Tenen, January 2004.

Kartchner family background: Author interviews with Mark and Dean Kartchner, January 2004. See also, Tufts, *History,* 5–6.

"We interviewed Mormons, we interviewed people who knew Mormons": Tenen interview.

"From our research, we were pretty sure": Ibid.

"Here we are going to tell them about it": Ibid.

Luray Caverns story: See Gurnee, *Discovery of Luray Caverns, Virginia,* 97–102. Also, Folsom, *Exploring American Caves,* 103–106.

First meeting with Kartchners: Tenen interview; also, Tufts, *History,* 25–26.

"The Kartchners were absolute people of their word": Tenen interview.

"They got along very well": Author interview with Dean Kartchner, January 2004.

"As we had agreed, the first priority is to build a working relationship": Randy Tufts and Gary Tenen letter to James Kartchner, March 8, 1978, Randy Tufts Collection, Arizona Historical Society.

"Because Xanadu is a live, active cave": Tufts and Tenen letter to James Kartchner, April 26, 1978, Tufts Collection.

"As if they lived intimately among the rocks and trees of the site": Randy Tufts taped interview with himself, June 13, 1989, courtesy of Gary Tenen.

"Both lean and skinny as rails": Dean Kartchner interview.

Dean Kartchner troubles in blowhole: Ibid.

"Mr. Kartchner was of pioneer stock": Tenen interview.

"When Dad was telling me about it": Randy Tufts taped interview with Max Kartchner, June 1989, Tufts Collection.

"It was freezing outside and we were all soaking wet": Tenen interview.

"It was great that we had the opportunity": Tufts taped interview with Paul Kartchner, May 1989, Tufts Collection.

CHAPTER SEVEN: LEWIS AND CLARK IN TUCSON

Gary Tenen meets Judy Quinlan: Author interview with Judy Tenen, June 2005.

"Please sign this letter to indicate your understanding": Secrecy agreement, courtesy of Gary Tenen.

"I had no idea what it was": Judy Tenen interview.

Laundromat episode: Ibid.

"We wanted to make sure they were old enough": Author interview with Dean Kartchner, January 2004.

"You had to change your clothes right there": Author interview with Kathy Kartchner, April 2006.

"We were crazy": Author interview with Gary Tenen, January 2004.

"Represented our trial by fire": Randy Tufts taped interview with himself, June 13, 1989, courtesy of Gary Tenen.

"We suspected the Kartchners didn't know much about caves": Ibid.

Four options for preserving the cave: Gary Tenen and Randy Tufts, *Cave Proposal,* 1978, 12–25.

"Go with your program": Tufts taped interview with himself.

Orion Knox cave mapping: Author interviews with Gary Tenen. See also, Tufts, *History,* 29–30.

"This guy crawls through the cave using his elbows": Randy Tufts taped interview with Gary Tenen, June 1989, Tufts Collection.

"I got the biggest set of blisters": Ibid.

"In walking through the new trail": Ibid.

"What was his name? . . . Mike Lewis": Tenen interview, January 2004.

"According to Roy Davis, some people would have been more willing": Tufts taped interview with himself.

"As you know I am involved in a project to develop a cave": Mike Lewis letter to Gary Roberson, October 13, 1979, Tufts Collection.

"All of us agreed that we wanted to turn it": Tenen interview.

The cave "became a part of living": Author interview with Max Kartchner, June 2005.

"Yes, there are two or three of them and they raise the IQ by 20 points": Tufts interview with Paul Kartchner, May 1989, Tufts Collection.

"It was a classic trip back to Americana": Tenen interview, January 2006.

"Within Mormon culture, the authority of the father is absolute": Ibid.

"For me, there were two discoveries in the course of this project": Tufts taped interview with himself.

"We planned together, we lived together, we shared together": Max Kartchner interview.

Kartchner Alaska cruise: Tufts, History, 33–34.

Cave interlopers: Kathy Kartchner interview; also, interviews with Tenen; also, Tufts, *History,* 34–35.

"You're not supposed to be doing this!" Kathy Kartchner interview.

"We gave him our word though and never went back": Author interview with Scott Davis, June 2005.

"We were all over the state" and **"Just another pretty cave":** Ibid.

CHAPTER EIGHT: THE YEARS IN THE WILDERNESS

Tufts visits Eatherly and shuts the door: Author interview with Charles Eatherly, February 2006. See also, Tufts, *History,* 36.

"I feel not trapped, enmeshed in a web of memories": Randy Tufts, 1983 journals, Randy Tufts Collection, Arizona Historical Society.

Master Dream List: Tufts Collection.

"The discovery of the cave [Xanadu] by others led me to fear for its safety": Tufts, 1983-1984 journals, Tufts Collection.

Outward Bound trip: Randy Tufts, "Outward Bound, October 4–26, 1984, Canyonlands National Park, Utah," written November 13, 1984, 1–35, Tufts Collection.

"When you're lost in the wild": Service, "The Quitter" in *Rhymes of a Rolling Stone,* 89.

"There were many times when I felt like stopping": Ibid.

McCullough visit: Randy Tufts taped interview with himself, June 13, 1989, courtesy of Gary Tenen.

Arizona spending on state parks: See Peterson, "Arizona, Long a Straggler on State Parks, Rushes to Catch Up," 8.

"A very sleepy place": Author interview with Bruce Babbitt, December 2005.

Babbitt and State Parks expansion: Price, *Gateways to the Southwest,* 111–139.

Tufts and Eatherly meet: Author interview with Charles Eatherly, February 2006. See also, Eatherly, *History of Arizona State Parks,* 41–42. For Tufts's perspective, see Tufts, *History,* 36.

Account of Eatherly blindfolded on trip to cave: Eatherly interview. See also, Eatherly, *History of Arizona State Parks,* 41–42.

Tenen and Tufts talk after Eatherly leaves: Tufts taped interview with himself.

"It was the best thing for the cave": Ibid.

"It is the most beautiful cave I have seen": Ed J. McCullough Jr. letter to Michael Ramnes, February 5, 1985.

"We'll put it on the list": Author interview with Gary Tenen, March 2006.

"Thanks Randy, we'll take it from here": Tufts, *History,* 38.

"The implication was that State Parks would handle everything": Tufts taped interview with himself.

Tufts visit to Arthur M. Young: Author interview with Carol Tufts and Judy Rodin, May 2005.

Tufts meeting with Carl Sagan: Randy Tufts letter to Gary Tenen and Brad Barber, August 20, 1977, Tufts Collection.

Meeting with Bruce Babbitt: Babbitt interview. See also, Tufts taped interview with himself and Tufts, *History,* 40.

"He was always the smartest person in the room": Author interview with Dan Campbell, June 2005.

Preparations for Babbitt visit: Tufts taped interview with himself.

"Scrambling down the hole": Babbitt interview.

"It was really incredible": Ibid.

"I now better understand and admire": Letter from Bruce Babbitt to Randy Tufts and Gary Tenen, April 17, 1985.

"They kept looking over their shoulders": Author interview with Bill Roe, June 2005.

Roe visit to cave: Ibid.

"We wanted to set the highest standard": Author interview with Gary Tenen, April 2006.

"When we buy things, we buy things expressly to protect them": Campbell interview.

"After hearing from Randy and Gary for years": Ibid.

"I didn't have the money personally": Babbitt interview.

Bud Cannon's humorous method of calculating cave value: H. C. "Bud" Cannon letter to Randy Tufts, June 9, 1989, Tufts Collection.

Buecher evaluation of caves: Letter "to whom it may concern" from Robert H. Buecher and Debbie S. Buecher, February 5, 1986, Tufts Collection.

"I want to tell you about a cave": Author interview with Steve Holland, January 2004.

Steve Holland, "CJ," and Scott Davis: Holland interview; also, Holland e-mail to author, March 2006.

Holland as "mole" and run-in with the Kartchners: Holland interview.

"It was the lesser of two evils": Ibid.

Randy Tufts's instructions in case of his death: Letter from Randy Tufts to Judy Tufts Rodin, November 20, 1985, courtesy of Judy Tufts Rodin.

CHAPTER NINE: THE STARS LINE UP

Randy in Hawaii: Randy Tufts account, "Volcano Hawaii," February 24, 1986, Randy Tufts Collection, Arizona Historical Society.

Hong Kong camera problems: Bill Peachey remembrance at Randy Tufts memorial service, 2002, videotape courtesy of Carol Tufts.

"Traveling my way has so far been highly introspective": Randy Tufts letter to Flo and Dave, July 12, 1986, Tufts Collection.

"We were feeling frustration and futility": Author interview with Mark Kartchner, January 2004.

"There are two guys in Tucson who you have to talk to": Author interview with Ken Travous, May 2005.

"They didn't know me from Adam": Ibid.

Travous and the rattlesnake: Related to author by Jay Ziemann, June 2005.

"My first thoughts": Travous interview.

"The tree was big and beautiful": Ibid.

"That is what got my attention": Author interview with Joe Lane, June 2005.

"We didn't have any major tourist destinations in southern Arizona": Ibid.

"Do I have to sign?": Author interview with Larry Hawke, May 2005.

"I'm not a racist": Quoted in Watkins, *High Crimes and Misdemeanors,* 73.

Mecham recall signatures: Berman, *Arizona Politics and Government,* 83.

"Every lawful means to oust Evan Mecham was in place": Watkins, *High Crimes and Misdemeanors,* 11.

Lane "had been the recipient of more abuse": Ibid, 301.

"In the legislature, nothing is secret": Lane interview.

"What we did—the three of us who knew": Ibid.

"The strategy was that we wanted as few people to know": Hawke interview.

Vehicle bill: Ibid.

"Weirdness can happen up there": Ibid.

"We didn't trust him or his minions": Lane interview.

"If Governor Mecham was interested in a new park in Arizona": Travous interview.

Dan Campbell meets with Kartchner brothers: Dan Campbell e-mail to author, September 23, 2005.

"I knew they had a large family": Ibid.

"A class act": Hawke interview.

"[T]he Kartchners were modest despite their significant achievements": Tufts, *History*, 68.

"You're right, Senator . . . There is a rat here": Travous interview.

Mecham trial before the Senate and conviction: Watkins, *High Crimes and Misdemeanors*, 319–358.

Pat Kossan and *Gazette* episode: Travous interview. Also, Tufts, *History*, 78.

"It was just a hole in the ground": Author interview with Dick Ferdon, May 2005.

Last-minute maneuverings surrounding Bill 1188: Travous interview and Hawke interview. Also, Tufts, *History*, 78–86.

"Mr. Chief Justice . . . this is not the way we normally conduct business": Tufts, *History*, 81.

"No wonder they found it": Ibid., 83.

The "silly season": Ibid.

"Hero medal": Lane interview.

"Ordinarily, I would have been opposed to how it was done": Author interview with John Kromko, January 2006.

"It was essentially a backroom deal": Author interview with Steve Holland, January 2004.

"If there had been anything other than impeachment going on": Lane interview.

As many as 40 percent of Republican primary voters were Mormons: Watkins, *High Crimes and Misdemeanors*, 178.

"It appears to me now that the stars were all lined up for this to happen": Travous interview.

"Well, it's done!": Author interview with Gary Tenen, January 2006.

"I want you guys to find a cave in my district now": Tufts, *History*, 84.

"This is as good as it ever gets for a bureaucrat": Ibid.

"We could finally tell people about it": Tenen interview.

CHAPTER TEN: FROM DESERT OUTPOST TO STATE PARK

Jim White and Carlsbad Caverns: See White, *Discovery and History of Carlsbad Caverns*.

"Everything was built with the idea of having one chance to do it right": Author interview with Jay Ream, June 2005.

ACPI background: Author interviews with Ron Bridgemon and Cindy Bethard, May 2005.

Conflict between Buecher and Tufts: Author interviews with Bob Buecher, June 2005 and Bill Peachey, January 2005.

"When we first started, we discovered we could not work together": Buecher interview, June 2005.

"The communications problems evident": Randy Tufts letter to Steve Holland, January 19, 1991 (not sent), Randy Tufts Collection, Arizona Historical Society.

"Buecher completed the project, but the checks and balances were gone": Author interview with Rafael Payan, June 2005.

"We were figuring out things like how many toilets": Author interview with Jeff Dexter, February 2006.

State Parks officials tossing around various ideas: Payan interview.

"The last big cave jobs were twenty and thirty years before": Dexter interview.

"Why not do it the old-fashioned way but do it very carefully": Payan interview.

"Much of our decision to put in horizontal tunnels and airlocks": Author interview with Rick Toomey, May 2005.

"It was extremely primitive": Dexter interview.

State Parks and Kartchner financial issues: Ream interview; author interview with Jay Ziemann, December 2006; and Price, *Gateways to the Southwest,* 159–163.

Giant squirt gun to cut the tunnels: Ream interview.

Blasting tunnels: Ream interview, Payan interview, and Dexter interview.

"Sitting underground while they were shooting explosives over my head": Dexter interview.

"One day we'd make ten feet": Payan interview.

"We had to rip out the whole side of the mountain": Ibid.

"Scraping the living daylights out of that hill": Author interview with Gary Tenen, January 2006.

Miners constantly leaving and **"Miners like a twenty-foot boom"**: Dexter interview.

"It was as if Randy and Gary were the parents": Author interview with Ken Travous, May 2005.

Travous as **"first rate public servant"**: Randy Tufts papers, November 1, 1995, Tufts Collection.

"With less and less contact with the project I worry about it": Ibid.

"So when I catch little snippets of difficulties at the cave, I worry": Ibid.

"We pretty much had to lock them out": Ream interview.

"My attitude was, 'State Parks bought it; it's theirs'": Tenen interview.

"Think about it. They have never done a cave before": Randy Tufts papers, November 1, 1995, Tufts Collection.

"Once those tunnels stopped and the cave began": Ream interview.

"Developing the cave is akin to capturing King Kong": Irwin, "Nature's Money Pit."

"We took a group of construction workers": Author interview with Ginger Nolan, May 2005.

"Horrendous turnover" and working at "cave's pace": Dexter interview.

"You got used to it" and "Everyone did whatever it took": Nolan interview.

"Everything we would do, we would do outside the cave": Payan interview.

"Everyone who goes into a cave leaves behind a belly button full of lint": Quoted in Blakeslee, "Glories of Underworld are Under Siege."

Carlsbad's lint problem: Hurd, *Entering the Stone*, 54.

"Consisted of lugging 600 feet of 8-inch-high pressure hose": Irwin, "Nature's Money Pit."

Unanticipated problems: wire, lubricant, saw, filters: Dexter interview.

"Once the water got high enough, we took the skinniest kid": Payan interview.

"The majority of the money to build the park came from Parks revenues": Author interview with Jay Ziemann, January 2006.

Kartchner and procurement code: Ibid.; also, Arizona State Parks Fact Sheet SB-1024 and Arizona House of Representatives Bill 2193.

"You develop a cave by 'yonders' and 'surelys'": Ziemann interview.

State Mine Inspector incident: Ziemann interview and Ream interview. Also, letter from Douglas K. Martin to Ken Travous, September 25, 1997. Also, letter from Ken Travous to Governor Jane Dee Hull, October 21, 1997. Also, see Benson, "Mine Inspector is Indicted on 9 Counts of Fraud, Theft."

Meeting at the cave with mine inspector's office: Dexter interview and Ziemann interview.

"If you don't do it our way, we'll walk": Related to author by Dexter.

"As long as we were building, we could collect funds from State Parks revenues": Payan interview.

Legislative "sunset review": Ziemann interview.

"Bewildering example of legislative short-sightedness": Editorial, "No Need to Rush."

"Delicate bit of God's handiwork": Letter from Governor Jane Dee Hull to Secretary of State Betsey Bayless, June 1, 1998.

Frank Florentine background: Author interview with Frank Florentine, November 2005.

"I saw that one drop could create a lot of noise": Ibid.

Account of approach to lighting the cave and problems: Ibid.

"You needed darkness to focus" and "Basically, it is all a big stage": Ibid.

Music in the cave and Tufts and Tenen: Tenen interview.

"If I had found it then . . . I would have done the logical thing": "Jewel of the Desert" video.

"I never saw a cave done so well": Related to author in Florentine interview.

CHAPTER ELEVEN: EPILOGUE

Tufts and Tenen meet with Ream at opening: Author interview with Jay Ream, June 2005.

"The cave is distinctly drier": Memo to Jay Ream regarding Environmental Issues at Kartchner, January 13, 2000, Randy Tufts Collection, Arizona Historical Society.

Statistics on temperature and humidity: Author interview with Rick Toomey, May 2005. See Arizona Conservation Projects, Inc. final report. Also, see Ingley, "Kartchner in Peril" and Stauffer, "Temps Creep Up."

Dryness in nearby caves: Toomey interview.

"After the opening of Throne/Rotunda, Gary and Randy read me the riot act": Ream interview.

"Take a sopping wet underground cavern": Blakeslee, "Glories of Underworld Are under Siege."

"Sincere commitment of Arizona State Parks": Tufts and Tenen, "Kartchner Caverns Stewards Must Elevate their Mission."

"To fix the immediate problems": Ibid.

"If Carlsbad can do 600,000": Quoted in Hogue, "Cochise Officials, Businesses Envision Mother Lode in Cave."

Multiplier effect on Benson: Ibid.

Benson census data: Jones, "CER Says Benson Growth Imminent."

Restaurant and bar sales up in Benson: Ibid.

Whetstone Springs plans: Tobin, "Park's Growing Pains Visiting Kartchner Caverns."

"A really bad idea": Quoted in Tobin, "Resort near Kartchner Raises Issue of Damage."

Newspaper editorials on subject: See Editorial: "Caverns Deserve Plenty of TLC," "Don't Cave In," "Kartchner: Be Careful," and "Kartchner Reprieve."

"If some yahoo at the resort": Quoted in Tobin, "Park's Growing Pains Visiting Kartchner Caverns."

"Aside from wishful thinking": Quoted in Tobin, "Benson Yet to Approve Luxury Resort near Caverns."

Tom Aley's experiment: Related by Jay Ziemann to author, January 2006.

Benson City Council public hearing: Description and all quotes in Tobin, "Benson Yet to Approve Luxury Resort near Caverns."

Arizona State Parks attempts to acquire property through eminent domain: Tobin, "State Acts to Gain Land near Kartchner."

Date and price of acquisition of property: E-mail to author from Ellen Bilbrey, Arizona State Parks, January 17, 2006.

"When Gary and I crawled into that cave": Quoted in Tobin, "Benson Yet to Approve Luxury Resort near Caverns."

"I want to study Europa:" Author interview with Richard Greenberg, June 2005.

"Randy would always say 'The Cave' when referring to Kartchner": Ibid. The account of Tufts's involvement with the Europa project comes from author conversation with Greenberg, June 2005.

Discussion of Jupiter fault discovery and ocean: see Wilford, "Scientists Point to New Evidence of Liquid Water on a Jupiter Moon"; Perlman, "Baffling Seismic Fault Seen in Icy Crust of Jovian Moon."

"It always seemed to me that if we found life someplace else": Quoted in Benson, "What Galileo Saw."

"When we humans find extraterrestrial life, wherever it is": Tufts, "Lithospheric Displacement Features on Europa and Interpretation," acknowledgements.

"Randy had obsessive goals": Greenberg interview.

Greenberg and Tufts trip to the Arctic: Greenberg e-mail to author, March 21, 2006.

Ericha Scott and Randy Tufts: Account of their meeting and relationship comes from author interviews with Ericha Scott Tufts, January 2004, May 2005, and January 2006.

"She is not as much of a flake as I thought": Ericha Scott Tufts remembrance of Randy Tufts at his memorial service, 2002.

Randy Tufts transplant: Account comes from Ericha Scott Tufts in interviews with the author. See also, McClain, "Sister's Marrow Reviving Kartchner Co-discoverer."

Carlos Valencia: Author conversations with Ericha Scott Tufts and Carol Tufts. See also, McClain, "A Fountain for Carlos."

"It was a very elegant presentation": Ericha Scott Tufts interview, May 2005.

Death of Randy Tufts: Author interviews with Ericha Scott Tufts, Carol Tufts, and Gary Tenen. See also, Martin, "Randy Tufts, Spelunker Who Kept a Secret, Is Dead at 53." Also, Negri, "Cave Discoverer's True Legacy."

Levi Tenen notices reactions to his father at Kartchner: Author interview with Levi Tenen, April 2003.

"Randy and Gary had such love for it:" Author interview with Rafael Payan, June 2005.

"But here was something you could really point to and be proud of": Author interview with Larry Hawke, May 2005.

"More experiences than I would have ever had otherwise": Author interview with Dean Kartchner, January 2004.

"Elvis in Disneyland" and "They set the bar high, and we set it two feet higher": Author interview with Ken Travous, May 2005.

Kartchner visitor figures: Fiscal year actuals, 2000–2006, Arizona State Parks.

"What effect will this have on the seventh generation to come?": Randy Tufts e-mail, May 24, 1996, Tufts Collection.

"Look at Kubla Khan. Drop by drop, moment by moment": Tufts papers, undated, Tufts Collection.

BOOKS

Abbey, Edward. *Desert Solitaire: A Season in the Wilderness.* New York: McGraw-Hill, 1968.

Berman, David R. *Arizona Politics and Government.* Lincoln: University of Nebraska Press, 1998.

Brucker, Roger W. and Richard A. Watson. *The Longest Cave.* New York: Alfred A. Knopf, 1976.

Cahalan, James M. *Edward Abbey: A Life.* Tucson: University of Arizona Press, 2001.

Church, Richard. *Five Boys in a Cave.* New York: The John Day Company, 1951.

Coleridge, Samuel Taylor. *The Portable Coleridge.* New York: The Viking Press, 1950.

Eatherly, Charles, ed. *History of Arizona State Parks* (Arizona State Parks internal document, unpublished).

Folsom, Franklin. *Exploring American Caves.* New York: Collier Books, 1962.

Gurnee, Russell H. *Discovery of Luray Caverns, Virginia.* Closter, NJ: R. H. Gurnee, Inc., 1978.

Hill, Carol A. and Paolo Forti. *Cave Minerals of the World.* Huntsville, AL: National Speleological Society, 1986.

Hurd, Barbara. *Entering the Stone.* Boston: Houghton Mifflin Company, 2003.

Jackson, Donald Dale and the Editors of Time-Life Books. *Underground Worlds.* Alexandria, VA: Time-Life Books, 1982.

McPhee, John. *Basin and Range.* New York: Farrar Straus Giroux, 1980.

Moore, George W. and Nicholas Sullivan. *Speleology: Caves and the Cave Environment.* St. Louis: Cave Books, 1997.

Murray, Robert K. and Roger W. Brucker. *Trapped!* New York: G. P. Putnam's Sons, 1979.

Negri, Sam. *Kartchner Caverns State Park.* Phoenix: Department of Transportation, State of Arizona, 1998.

Price, Jay M. *Gateways to the Southwest: The Story of Arizona State Parks.* Tucson: University of Arizona Press, 2004.

Service, Robert W. *Rhymes of a Rolling Stone*. New York: Dodd, Mead, & Co., 1912.

Sonnichsen, C. L. *Tucson, The Life and Times of an American City*. Norman: University of Oklahoma Press, 1982.

Tufts, Randy. *History of Kartchner Caverns*. Unpublished, 1989.

Tufts, Bruce Randall. "Lithospheric Displacement Features on Europa and Interpretation." Ph.D. dissertation, Department of Geosciences, University of Arizona, 1998.

Watkins, Ronald J. *High Crimes and Misdemeanors: The Term and Trials of Former Governor Evan Mecham*. New York: William Morrow & Co., 1990.

White, James Larkin. *The Discovery and History of Carlsbad Caverns*. Carlsbad, New Mexico: Carlsbad Caverns Guadeloupe Mountains Association, copyright 1932, reprinted 1998.

ARTICLES

An Introduction to the Escabrosa Grotto, 1970s, undated.

Benson, Matthew. "Mine Inspector Is Indicted on 9 Counts of Fraud, Theft," *Arizona Republic,* December 15, 2006.

Benson, Michael. "What Galileo Saw," *The New Yorker,* September 8, 2003.

Blakeslee, Sandra. "Glories of Underworld Are under Siege; Science Armed a Cave for Its Public Debut," *New York Times,* September 5, 2000.

Brown, Roland. "Onyx Events Calendar," *Desert Caver,* 4, no. 4 (December 1974).

Cahill, Tim. "The CO_2 Chronicles," *National Geographic Adventure,* 5, no. 9 (November 2003).

Editorial. "Caverns Deserve Plenty of TLC," *Arizona Republic,* July 15, 2001.

———. "Don't Cave In," *Arizona Daily Star,* July 6, 2001.

———. "Kartchner: Be Careful," *Arizona Daily Star,* July 1, 2001.

———. "Kartchner Reprieve," *Arizona Daily Star,* September 7, 2001.

———. "No Need to Rush," *Arizona Republic,* May 26, 1998.

Gurnee, Russell H. "Conservation through Commercialization: The Rio Camuy Cave Project, Puerto Rico," *Bulletin of the National Speleological Society,* 29, no. 2 (April 1967).

Hogue, RuthAnn. "Cochise Officials, Businesses Envision Mother Lode in Cave," *Arizona Daily Star,* November 8, 1999.

Holland, Steve. "The Frustrated Caver's Guide to Finding Secret Caves in Arizona," *Desert Caver,* 9, no. 2 (June 1979).

Ingley, Kathleen. "Kartchner in Peril," *Arizona Republic,* September 6, 2000.

Irwin, Dave. "Nature's Money Pit," *Tucson Weekly,* April 23–28, 1998.

Jones, Ken. "CER Says Benson Growth Imminent," *San Pedro Valley News-Sun,* July 4, 2001.

Kimble, Mark. "Beyond Colossal," *Tucson Citizen,* March 11, 2004.

Martin, Doug. "Randy Tufts, Spelunker Who Kept a Secret, Is Dead at 53," *New York Times,* April 21, 2002.

McClain, Carla. "A Fountain for Carlos," *Arizona Daily Star,* February 11, 2005.

———. "Sister's Marrow Reviving Kartchner Co-discoverer," *Arizona Daily Star,* November 27, 2000.

Negri, Sam. "Cave Discoverer's True Legacy," *Arizona Daily Star,* April 3, 2002.

Perlman, David. "Baffling Seismic Fault Seen in Icy Crust of Jovian Moon," *San Francisco Examiner,* December 8, 1998.

Peterson, Iver. "Arizona, Long a Straggler on State Parks, Rushes to Catch Up," *New York Times,* December 7, 1985.

Simonson, Scott. "'New Cave Yields Deep Secrets," *Arizona Daily Star,* March 12, 2004, B1.

Stauffer, Thomas. "Temps Creep Up: Kartchner Caverns Gets Warmer, Drier," *Arizona Daily Star,* February 9, 2003.

Tobin, Mitch. "Benson Yet to Approve Luxury Resort near Caverns," *Arizona Daily Star,* September 6, 2001.

———. "Park's Growing Pains Visiting Kartchner Caverns," *Arizona Daily Star,* July 26, 2001.

———. "Resort near Kartchner Raises Issue of Damage," *Arizona Daily Star,* June 29, 2001.

———. "State Acts to Gain Land near Kartchner," *Arizona Daily Star,* January 11, 2002.

Tufts, Randy and Gary Tenen. "Kartchner Caverns Stewards Must Elevate their Mission," *Arizona Republic,* September 17, 2000.

Wilbur, Richard E. "Uranium Rush Moves Closer to Tucson," *Tucson Citizen,* February 19, 1976.

Wilford, John Noble. "Scientists Point to New Evidence of Liquid Water on a Jupiter Moon," *New York Times,* September 17, 1999.

Page numbers appearing in **boldface** refer to illustrations.

Agenbroad, Larry, 160
Aley, Tom, 158, 173
Angel's Wing formation, 47, **61**, 84, 120
aragonite crystal, 25
Arizona Conservation Projects, Inc. (ACPI), 140–43
Arizona Nature Conservancy, 106, 109, 110, 124; and Heritage Fund, 148; *modus operandi*, 106–7, 128
Arizona-Sonora Desert Museum, 87, 95
Arizona State Parks, 184; acquires property by eminent domain, 174; financial difficulties, 147–48; receives presentation by Tufts and Tenen, 102; role in cave development, 139–65; "sunset" review of, 161; and Tufts's visit, 95; under pressure over drying caverns, 171

Babbitt, Bruce, 105, 117; interest in transforming Arizona State Parks, 98; meeting with Tufts, Tenen, and Mark Kartchner, 104–5; offer to raise money, 109; visit to Kartchner, 106
Barber, Brad, 18, 39
bats (*Myotis velifer*), 39, **39**, 108, 142
Benson (Arizona), 36, 122, 167; and expected economic windfall, 171; and proposed resort, 173–74
Big Room (at Kartchner), 29, 37, **107**; opening of, 181; tunnel into, 150–51

Blanchard Springs (Arkansas), 101, 140, 145
blowhole, 6, **8**, 70, **113**
Bolding, Betsy, 104, 106
Bridgemon, Ron, 26, 140
Buecher, Bob, 24, 26, 142 **143**; and Babbitt visit, 105; differences with Tufts, 142–43; as project manager of ACPI, 140, 144; and "ratings" of caves, 110; on secrecy, 55
Buecher, Debbie, 106, 110, 142, **143**
Burch, Jack, 85, 86, 146

Campbell, Dan, 107, 109, 110; impression of Babbitt, 105; initial misgivings, 108; negotiations with Kartchners, 128–29
Carlsbad Caverns (New Mexico), 41, 59, 101, 110, 122; discovery of and early tourism at, 139; evaporation at, 146; and lint, 158; mistakes in development of, 139–40; raccoon problem at, 140
cave bacon, **29**, 30, **30**, **103**
Cave of the Bells, 15, 25, 26
Cave Research Foundation, 26, 140, 142
Caverns of Sonora (Texas), 59, 82, 84, 110; Tenen work experience at, 84–86
caving and caving practices, 10, 21–24
Church of Jesus Christ of Latter-day Saints (Mormons), 64, 89, 125, 136
Clark, Bob. *See* Tufts, Randy: use of pseudonym
Coleridge, Samuel Taylor, 34, 48
Collins, Floyd, 23

Colossal Cave (Arizona), 13, 41, 56, 168

Crackerjack (CJ, early name for Kartchner Caverns), 93, 112. *See also* Kartchner Caverns; Xanadu

Cul de Sac Passage (Kartchner Caverns), 37, **91**

Davis, Roy, 84, 86

Davis, Scott, 54, 112–13, 115; enters Xanadu, 92–93

Desert Caver, 26, 55–56

Dexter, Jeff, 144, **145**, 152, 158–59; on early state of Kartchner, 146; and tests dynamiting in cave, 150; on employee turnover, 157

Discovery Center (Kartchner), 146, 154, 165, **168, 169**, 182

drying/evaporation: in Kartchner Caverns, 167–71

Duncan, Chuck, **156**

Eatherly, Charles, 98, **99**, 118; meets Tufts, 95; and lack of support, 102; visits cave, 100–102

Emery, Jean, 174

Escabrosa Grotto, 3, 26, 52, 53–56

Ferdon, Dick, 133, 138

Fife, John, 179

Five Boys in a Cave, 13, 96

Florentine, Frank: and lighting of cave, 162–64; praised by Tenen, 165

food: in caves, 36, 139

Forest Service (USDA), 53, 54; and lack of cave protection, 25

fried egg formation, 30, **32**

Gill, Eric, 29

Gordon, Francis X., 130, 134

Greenberg, Richard, 175, 176; and trip with Tufts to Arctic, 177

Groscost, Jeff, 161–62

Gurnee, Russell, 57, 146

Hawke, Larry, 124–25, **124**, 126, 127, 129, 132, 134, 135; on legislative "weirdness," 128; on pride in Kartchner, 182; on "vehicle bill," 127

Hawke, Tommy, 124–25

Hays, John, 124, 126, 127, 132, 135

helictites, **22**, 47, 85, **111**

Heritage Fund, 148, 161

Herschend, Bruce, 154–55

Holland, Steve, **113**, 143; and "discovery" of cave site, 112–13; infiltrates cave interlopers, 114–15; on legislative tactics, 136; pens parody of grotto secrecy culture, 55–56

Horseshoe Café (Benson), 36, 63, 82, 84, 99–100, 171

Howe Caverns (New York), 59, 60

Hull, Jane Dee, 161, 165

Irwin, Dave, 155, 158

Kartchner, Dean, 67, 68, 69, **89**, 95, 115, 135; and affect of cave, 182; struggles to enter cave, 69–70; on secrecy, 79

Kartchner, Dwight, 70

Kartchner, Fred, 68, 69, **72**

Kartchner, Glen, 68

Kartchner, James A., 61, 64, **65**, 70, 72; anniversary party, 88–89; approached by Tufts and Tenen "agent," 62; death of, 117; first cave visit, 68, 70; meets Tufts and Tenen, 66–67; second cave visit, 88

Kartchner, Kathy, 79; discovers Xanadu intruders, 92

Kartchner, Kevin, 70

Kartchner, Lois, 64, **65**, 66–67, 78, 88, 137; and cave photo, 138

Kartchner, Mark, 63, 65, 68, 89, 104

Kartchner, Max, 63, 65, 68, 73, 88, 89, 92, 137; meets Dick Ferdon, 133–34

Kartchner, Milo, 70

Kartchner, Paul, 68, 69, 73, 88, 89

Kartchner Caverns: appraisal of, 109–12, 118, 121, 128–29; delays in construction, 147; and development inside cave, 154–59; drying in, 167–71; early days as state park, 167; financial issues, 147; future of, 184; geologic history of, 37–38; grand opening of, 165; history of property, 63; and legislative issues during construction, 159–60, 161; and legislative strategy to acquire, 126–37; lighting of, 162–64; map of,

10; naming of park, 129; number of visitors to, 183; and role of women during construction, 157; and travails of workers, 157; and trespassing attempts, 149–52. *See also* Crackerjack; Xanadu

Kartchner family, 64; accepts state terms for purchase, 129; on Alaskan cruise, 90; bond with Tufts and Tenen, 88, 89; brothers ward off trespassers, 114; first cave visit, 68; initiation into secrecy, 79–80; meeting with Travous, 121; other peoples' views of family, 129; plan to seal entrance, 118; as "superior species," 88; withdrawal from plans for development of cave, 90

Knox, Orion, 77, **83**, cave-mapping techniques, 84; consultation on Kartchner development, 145; conversation with Tenen, 82; visit to cave, 82, 84

Kossan, Pat, 132–33

Kromko, John, 15, 16, 18; admiration for Tufts 19, 136

Kubla Khan (formation), 34, **45**, 48; lighting of, 163–64

"Kubla Khan" (poem), 34, 48

Kunasek, Carl, 122, 134

Lane, Joe, 121–22, 133, 135; on cave legislative strategy, 126–27; defeat in primary, 136; on impeachment as factor in cave approval, 136; on Mecham, 128; role in impeachment, 126; sees photos of cave, 122; on Ken Travous, 136

Larson, Lane, 93

legislative strategy, 126–27

Lewis, Mike. *See* Tenen, Gary: use of pseudonym

lighting (at Kartchner), 162–64, 165

Longest Cave, The (Brucker and Watson), 23

Luray Caverns (Virginia), 66, 84, 140; music at, 164; and Tenen work experience, 86

Mammoth Cave (Kentucky), 59, 110, 122, 158

Martin, Douglas K., 160

McCullough, Ed, 97–98, 106; writes to Parks director, 102

Mecham, Evan, 117, 125; controversial views, 125; impeachment trial and conviction of, 125–26, 130, 132; kept in the dark on cave 125

media coverage, 132–35, 155, 158, 161–62, 165, 167, 170–71, 173

Merlin's (Tucson student bar), 18–19, 26

mining: threat of, 51

Mofford, Rose, 132, 135–36, **137**

Mormons. *See* Church of Jesus Christ of Latter-day Saints

mud, 36, 42–43, 47, 79, 84, 159

mud trench, 42, 47, 70

Mushroom Passage (Kartchner), **10**, **53**, **123**

music, in Throne Room complex, 163

National Caves Association (NCA), 60, 78, 82

National Environmental Policy Act, 21

National Speleological Society (NSS), 24, 26

Natural Bridge Caverns (Texas), 82, 146

Nelson, Cortland, 122, 133

Nolan, Ginger, 156–57

Northway, Steve, 34, 36

Onyx Cave (Arizona), 24, 25, 26, 51, 54, 56, 80

Payan, Rafael, 146, 157, 158, 161; on Big Room tunnel, 150–51; as part of development triumvirate, 144; on Tufts and Tenen's role, 152, 153

Peachey, Bill, 26, 56; almost identifies "Mike Lewis," 86; on Arizona caving culture, 21, 23–24; discovery of La Tetera, 56; seals cave entrance, 57; on Tufts and Tenen, 21, 27

Peppersauce Cave (Arizona), 24, **25**; and vandalism, 64, 67, 79

Ream, Jay, 140, 147, 153, 155; on development conflicts, 153; on drying in caverns, 167, 169–70

rimstone dams, **38**

River Passage (Kartchner), 37, 42

Rodin, Judy Tufts, 115; as transplant donor, 179

Roe, Bill, **109**; meeting with Tufts and Tenen, 107; negotiations with Kartchners, 108–9; visits cave, 107–8

Rotunda Room, 47, **85**; lighting of, 162–64; open to public, 164–65

Rotunda–Throne Room complex: development of, 155

Ruff, Howard: financial advice, 90

Sagan, Carl, 104, 175, 177

St. David (Arizona), 61–63, 66, 88

San Xavier del Bac (mission church), 161

secrecy, 77–79; document, **83**

Senate Bill 1188, 127, 130, 132–33, 135, 147. *See also* "vehicle bill"

Service, Robert W.: poetry of, 97

Shelf Passage, **37**, **131**

Shover, Bill, 133

Siddha Yoga Center, 177

soda straw formations, 7, **9**, 12, 29, **35**, **53**, **111**, **123**, 131; second-longest in world, **46**, 47–48, 84, 148

Southside Presbyterian Church (Tucson), 179

speleothems, 24, 40, 139, 168

Strawberry Room, 34, **35**, **43**, **101**

Taylor, Jack, 130

Tenen, David, 95, 177

Tenen, Gary, 14; AlphaGraphics, 96; appeal of caving, 15, 180; attends vote to approve cave, 134–35; birth of children, 95; caught in River Passage drop, 42–43, 47; and cave development process, 152–54; on cave lighting, 165; and caving gear, 36; confronts trespassers, 92–93; and conversation with Orion Knox, 82; discovery of Big Room, 29–31; discovery of Red Cave, 15; discovery of Xanadu, 3–12; on drying caverns, 167–71, 184; early dealings with Arizona State Parks, 97–104; early friendship with Randy Tufts, 16; early visits to Xanadu, 29–49; encounter with bats, 39; family

life, 177; first caving trip, 15; and grand-opening ceremony, 165; hiding presence at cave, 52–53; on hiring cave scientist, 171; indirect approach to Mr. Kartchner, 62; on Kartchner development conflicts, 153; and Kartchner legislation, 138; legacy of conservation ethic, 182–83; marriage to Judy Quinlan, 78; meeting with Bill Roe, 107; meeting with Kartchners, 63; meeting with Ken Travous, 118–19; and passage of Bill 1188, 137; personality differences with Randy Tufts, 14, 61; presentation of proposal to Kartchner family, 80; use of pseudonym ("Mike Lewis"), 77–78, 82, 86–87; relationship with Kartchners, 88, 89; research into Kartchner family, 62; reticence at Grotto meetings, 27; on searching for caves, 15; saves Tufts's life, 4; secrecy regarding cave discovery, 52; as steward of Kartchner Caverns, 181; and student activism, 16–17; takes Charles Eatherly to cave, 99–101; takes Governor Babbitt to cave, 106; trips with Kartchners to cave, 68–70, 73, 88; on secrecy, 80; and visit from Steve Holland, 112; work at Sonora and Luray Caverns, 84–87; working relationship with Randy Tufts, 61; worries about Xanadu vulnerability, 51

Tenen, Judy Quinlan, 88, 137, 152; early relationship with Gary, 78; views on secrecy, 78–79, 95

Tenen, Julia, 95, 177

Tenen, Levi, 95, 177, 182

Throne Room, **44**, **45**, 47, 84, 111, **172**

Tonto Natural Bridge, 147–48

Toomey, Rick: as cave resource manager, 171; on evaporation at Carlsbad, 146

Travous, Kenneth, **119**, 162, 171, 173; calls on legislators, 122–23; celebrates victory in legislature, 136–37, 138; conflict with mine inspectors, 161; conflict with news media, 132–33; conflict with Tufts and Tenen over development,

152–53; early years, 121; as "Elvis in Disneyland," 182; encounter with rattlesnake, 119; first visit to cave, 119; legislative maneuverings, 130; on music for cave tour, 164; as State Parks executive director, 118. *See also* Lane, Joe

trespassing, 90, 92–93, 114–15

Tucson (Arizona): caving community in, 23, 26; fast-growing nature of, 52; in 1960s, 16; landscape, 21

Tufts, Carol, 14, 17

Tufts, Ericha Scott, **179**, 181; meets and marries Randy Tufts, 177–80; and Randy's illness, 179–81

Tufts, Pete, 14, 104

Tufts, Randy, 14; activities at University of Arizona, **17**, 17–19; anxiety about Kartchner development, 152–54; attends vote to approve cave, 134–35; and cave development process, 152–54; and caving gear, 36; confronts trespassers, 92–93; death of, 181; differences with Bob Buecher, 142–44; discovery of Big Room, 29–31; discovery of Red Cave, 15; discovery of Xanadu, 3–12; on drying caverns, 167–71, 184; early dealings with Arizona State Parks, 97–104; early friendship with Gary Tenen, 16; encounter with bats, 39; fascination with caves, 13–14; first visits to Xanadu, 29–49; graduate studies at University of Arizona, 154, 174–77; and grand-opening ceremony, 165; hiding presence at cave, 52–53; on hiring cave scientist, 171; hitchhiking across country, 59–60; and illness, 177, 179–81; indirect approach to Mr. Kartchner, 62; initial visit to Arizona State Parks, 95, 97–98; involvement with Merlin's, 18–19; last instructions, 115; legacy of conservation ethic, 182–83; meeting with Bill Roe, 107; meeting with Ken Travous, 118–19; meets and marries Ericha Scott, 179–180; meets Kartchners, 63; move to Denver, 96; move to

Tucson, 60; Outward Bound trip, 95–96; and passage of Bill 1188, 137; personality differences with Gary Tenen, 14, 61; presentation of proposal to Kartchner family, 80; use of pseudonym ("Bob Clark"), 77; relationship with Kartchners, 88, 89; relationship with Tenens, 177; research into Kartchner family, 62; reticence at Grotto meetings, 27; reverence for cave, 48–49, 184; on searching for caves, 15; sense of humor, 179, 180; takes Charles Eatherly to cave, 99–101; takes Governor Babbitt to cave, 106; testimony at Benson public hearing, 174, 180–81; travels around the world, 117–18; trips with Kartchners to cave, 68–70, 73; trip to Colossal Cave, 13; works for Tucson Public Power, 26; working relationship with Gary Tenen, 61; worries about Xanadu vulnerability, 51

Turnip formation, **48**

University of Arizona, 13, 92, 98, 154, 177; in the 1960s, 16; Tufts's research at, 174–76; student politics at, 17–18

vandalism: of caves, 24–26, **25**, 29, 51, 54, 57, 102

"vehicle bill," 126–28, 130, 132. *See also* Senate Bill 1188

Wade, Steve, 5

Wade's Cave, 5, 6

Walker, Harry, 5, 13, 24, 48, 60

Watkins, Ronald J., 125–26

Whetstone Mountains, 3, **4**, 51, 82, 168

Whetstone Springs proposed development, 173–74

White, Jim, 139

Williams, Jack, 26

Xanadu (early name for Kartchner Caverns): ascents and descents, 42; and Coleridge poem, 34; contrast to Colossal Cave and Carlsbad Caverns, 40–41; living quality of,

Xanadu, *continued*
40; mud trench 42; naming of,
34; spiritual significance of, 73;
vulnerability of, 51, 57. *See also*
Crackerjack; Kartchner Caverns

Ziemann, Jay: confrontation with
mine inspector, 161; Kartchner
exemption from procurement
code, 159–60; legislative tours, 159

Neil Miller is a lecturer in journalism and nonfiction writing at Tufts University in Medford, Massachusetts. He is a former staff writer at the *Boston Phoenix*. His articles have appeared in the *Boston Globe Magazine*, the *Los Angeles Times*, the *Washington Post*, and a number of other publications.

He is the author of four nonfiction books, including *In Search of Gay America: Women and Men in a Time of Change* (Atlantic Monthly Press, 1989), which was the winner of the 1990 American Library Association prize for gay and lesbian nonfiction. His most recent work, *Sex-Crime Panic: A Journey to the Paranoid Heart of the 1950s* (Alyson Books, 2002), received the 2003 Randy Shilts Award for nonfiction and was designated a 2003 Stonewall Honor Book by the American Library Association.

Mr. Miller lives in Somerville, Massachusetts.

Library of Congress Cataloging-in-Publication Data

Miller, Neil, 1945–
Kartchner Caverns : how two cavers discovered
and saved one of the wonders of the natural world /
Neil Miller.
p. cm.
Includes bibliographical references and index.
ISBN 978-0-8165-2516-4 (pbk. : alk. paper)
1. Kartchner Caverns State Park (Ariz.)
2. Tufts, Randy. 3. Tenen, Gary.
4. Spelunkers—Arizona—Tucson—Biography. I. Title.
GV200.655.A62 K375 2008
796.52'50922—dc22
[B]   2007021535